Tony Gardiner

MORE MATHEMATICAL CHALLENGES

CAMBRIDGE
UNIVERSITY PRESS

PUBLISHED BY THE PRESS SYNDICATE OF THE UNIVERSITY OF CAMBRIDGE
The Pitt Building, Trumpington Street, Cambridge CB2 1RP, United Kingdom

CAMBRIDGE UNIVERSITY PRESS
The Edinburgh Building, Cambridge CB2 2RU, United Kingdom
40 West 20th Street, New York, NY 10011-4211, USA
10 Stamford Road, Oakleigh, Melbourne 3166, Australia

First published 1997

Printed in the United Kingdom at the University Press, Cambridge

Typeset in 10.5/13pt Times

A catalogue record for this book is available from the British Library

ISBN 0 521 58568 6   paperback

CONTENTS

Solving problems is a practical art, like swimming, or skiing, or playing the piano: . . . if you wish to learn swimming you have to go into the water, and if you wish to become a problem-solver you have to solve problems.

George Polya

Introduction

Teachers are increasingly concerned to find materials that can be used to extend their more able pupils. Should such pupils move on to more advanced topics (as the levels structure of the English National Curriculum implicitly advocates)? Or should they explore elementary topics in greater depth, achieving fluency and flexibility in working with relatively simple material? There is no easy answer. Some pupils are clearly ready for harder topics (fractions, ratios, similarity, algebra, trigonometry) earlier than other pupils; but systematic 'vertical' acceleration for individuals or small groups (as opposed to whole classes) can cause severe administrative, and sometimes even social, problems. On the other hand, a consistent strategy of 'horizontal' extension demands that teachers be familiar with suitable extension material for all ages, and in a form that can be easily used by individuals or small groups within a class.

This collection of over 160 elementary but challenging problems for able youngsters (age 11–15) should be of interest to all mathematics teachers, irrespective of the particular strategy they use to extend their able pupils. The book – with its problems, comments and hints, and outline solutions – may be used either by teachers as an occasional resource or directly by individual pupils. Most of the problems come from the 1989–95 papers of the UK Junior Mathematical Olympiad (JMO) – an event which seeks to challenge, to stimulate and to encourage large numbers of able youngsters from all kinds of schools. There is also a section containing 60 additional problems of the same kind.

The problems in the UK JMO, and hence the kinds of solutions expected, are *mathematical*; but they must also be accessible to many talented pupils who have as yet very limited technical training. Accessibility is achieved in part by using settings which are elementary or informal – involving numbers, cubes, clocks, calendars, balls, pipes, etc. However, the instructions to candidates make it clear that this should not be misconstrued as encouraging 'informal' solutions. Informal settings allow more pupils to get started on a problem; but any acceptable mathematical solution must interpret the problem in a way that highlights its key *mathematical* features, and then uses these clearly, deductively and effectively.

The problems are arranged in fifteen groups. Each of the 1990–95 papers has two parts – a Section A and a Section B; the 1989 paper is essentially one long Section B. There are also 60 'additional' problems – 40 Section A and 20 Section B problems.

Section A questions are direct, 'closed' problems, each requiring a specific calculation and having a single numerical answer. Early Section A questions (A1, A2) tend to be relatively straightforward: for example,

> **1994, A1:** What is the angle between the hands of a clock at 9:30?

Later Section A questions (A7–A10) can be rather hard: for example,

> **1993, A10:** In how many different ways can one pay 20p using standard British coins (1p, 2p, 5p, 10p, 20p)?

Able pupils can often divine the answers to such problems in inscrutable ways. But mathematics is about *reasons*, not just answers. Thus, when using Section A problems, teachers should insist that the relevant calculation be presented clearly – so that, in particular, errors can be located and corrected.

Section B questions are longer and more 'open'. Thus, while the final mathematical solution is often quite short, and should involve a clear claim, followed by a direct deductive calculation or proof, there will generally be a preliminary phase of exploration and conjecture, in which one tries to sort out how to tackle the problem. Here is an example:

> **1993, B2:** 31.3.93 is an 'interesting' date, since $31 \times 3 = 93$. How many years of the twentieth century contain no interesting dates at all?

Some exploration and thought is clearly needed to find an approach which will allow one to count such years in a reliable and easily explained way. This activity is important; but it is *pre*-mathematical. The mathematics of the problem lies chiefly in identifying and presenting a convincing deductive analysis which solves the problem. Thus, in Section B problems, pupils (and teachers) should never be content with an 'answer', even if it is supported by rough work. Instead these problems should be used as a way of learning to organise, and to present mathematical calculations, or chains of reasoning, in a way which explains clearly *why* the answer is what it is.

Mathematics is not about mere answers; it is the science of *how to* calculate and *how to* reason correctly. Thus, in counting years with no interesting dates, a numerical answer is wholly unconvincing – even if it happens to be correct. A list of 100 years – each followed by a tick or a cross – is not much better, since it leaves to the reader all the work of checking, for example, whether any of the crosses should in fact be ticks. For an acceptable solution, what is needed is a short, clearly expressed and totally convincing chain of *reasons* that explains why all but a handful of years can be immediately excluded, and which then checks each of the years that remain.

As in Section A, *early* Section B questions (B1, B2) tend to be more accessible than later questions (B5, B6).

A good mathematics problem can always be adapted for use with a much wider group than that for which it was originally designed. It would be nice to think that teachers will take such liberties with this material too. It would be even nicer if those who do so would try to preserve its explicitly *mathematical* spirit.

Finally I should acknowledge my debt to Zad Khan, whose painstaking efforts have helped to eliminate many of the errors in earlier versions of this book. The unusual format (especially of the outline solutions) has been chosen to prevent passive reading: I would welcome comments from readers who see other – possibly better – ways of achieving the same objective.

To the reader

These problems are intended to stretch and to challenge able youngsters, whatever their background. Pupils must be prepared to find the problems hard, and be willing to struggle to solve them. Provided they struggle intelligently, they should experience both a measure of success and the satisfaction of learning valuable lessons from grappling with those problems that stump them.

Able pupils can easily be misled into thinking that mathematics is 'easy'. It isn't. Mathematical problems *can* be solved; but they do not always yield up their secrets easily. And often, even when one thinks one knows what the answer must be, a lot of work is needed to discover a *proof*.

For most of the problems in this book pupils will already be familiar with the mathematical ingredients needed for a solution. But these are challenging problems, not mere exercises, so one must expect to have to do more than simply apply some known formula or method. In particular, pupils must be prepared

- first to *interpret* the problem;
- then to *select* an appropriate technique; and
- finally
  - (a) in Section A problems to perform the relevant *calculation* correctly to obtain the required answer, and
  - (b) in Section B problems to identify the heart of the matter, and then to present a *general solution* (for example, using algebra, or a logical proof).

Provided one is familiar with the necessary techniques, the stages outlined above are, as Einstein once observed, 'refined common sense'. This does not make them easy! The challenge of mathematics lies chiefly in coordinating simple ingredients to achieve a correct solution. In particular, pupils should

4

not dash from one half-solved problem to the next, but should concentrate on trying to write out full and correct solutions to a small number of problems, and (by consulting the *Comments and hints*, and the *Outline solutions*) learn as much as possible from tackling each problem.

To avoid misunderstandings, it is important to stress that

> *all the problems are meant to be done without a calculator.*

In particular, all calculations should be *correct* (manipulating numbers and symbols correctly, and using '=' to mean 'truly equal to') and *exact* (for example, avoiding estimates, and using fractions and surds rather than decimals).

Guesswork can be useful in private, but should never form part of a final solution. Mathematics may involve experimentation, but it is *not* an experimental science. Though it can be helpful when working in rough to 'spot a pattern', a final solution must obtain the conjectured answer *deductively*. Thus, one must somehow find a *logical* reason why the answer has to be what one thinks it is. Experimental evidence proves nothing. In particular, a guess cannot be justified by checking a few cases; and geometry problems can never be solved by measuring on a scale diagram. Mathematical conclusions must be based on *general proofs*.

Mathematics remains reliable only in so far as its calculations and deductions are strictly *logical* – that is, based on precise mathematical reasoning. In contrast, experimental evidence is mainly *psychological*. Checking a few cases may make one *feel* more confident (something that can be psychologically useful in that it helps keep one going); but it is mathematically worthless. Experimental evidence and precise mathematical reasoning are related in much the same way as darkness and light: they go together, but are in some sense *opposites*, and should certainly never be confused. Mathematical enlightenment depends on knowing which one is the final arbiter.

The central position of mathematics in the modern world and in human culture stems from its being the only 'exact science'. Moreover, the usefulness and power of mathematics arise from the fact that the complicated answers and expressions which its exact methods throw up can often be *simplified* in a way that transforms an incomprehensible morass of symbols into something magically familiar. In mathematics, *meaning* depends on simplification, which in turn depends on *robust technique*. At the heart of all

5

mathematics there lies a determination to find meaning in otherwise meaningless expressions. In particular, one should never accept answers like

$$12^2 + 1 - 145, \quad \text{or} \quad \frac{192}{384}, \quad \text{or} \quad \frac{\dfrac{x+1}{x-1} + 1}{\dfrac{x+1}{x-1} - 1}$$

if the true answer is 0, or $\frac{1}{2}$, or x. The above expressions may be 'formally correct', but they remain unsimplified, and hence uncomprehended.

Within the context of the UK JMO pupils work on their own, and under a severe time constraint. This is an important part of the challenge. A group of average ability faced with the problem

> **1994, A1** What is the angle between the hands of a clock at 9:30?

will realise, after some discussion, that the answer is not 90°, and should succeed eventually in finding the correct value. More able students should be expected to work such things out quickly, and correctly, in their heads.

In the absence of a time constraint, many pupils may be tempted to tackle problem

> **1993, A10** In how many ways can one pay 20p using standard British coins?

by laboriously drawing up a list of all the different ways of making 20p. As I have explained, able pupils should realise that such an approach is inadequate, in that it is rarely sufficiently systematic to be reliable. Imposing a time constraint emphasises the crucial fact that mathematics must be based on *insight*, and on *exact calculation*, not on optimistic, but unreliable, trial-and-error.

The Junior Olympiad papers
1989–95

These problems are meant to be tackled *without the use of calculators*, and without measuring.

Solutions to Section A questions should consist of a clearly presented, and exact, calculation leading to a numerical answer.

Section B questions usually involve a degree of exploration, which is not part of the final solution. These are *not* 'investigations', and your solutions should *not* look like an investigation report ('This is what I did', 'This is what I found', 'These are my conclusions'). Solutions to Section B questions are often quite short, and should be presented *logically*, with clear explanations and proofs.

Answers and calculations should always be *exact* – using symbols, fractions, or surds where appropriate, not decimal approximations. Answers should also always be in *fully simplified form*.

When you get well-and-truly stuck on a problem, look first at the comment in the *Comments and hints* section. If you remain stuck, consult the *Outline solutions*.

1995: Section A

A1 Evaluate $123\,123 \div 1001$.

A2 What is the size of the angle x in the diagram on the right?

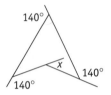

A3 What is $\dfrac{1}{1 \times 2} + \dfrac{1}{2 \times 3} + \dfrac{1}{3 \times 4} + \dfrac{1}{4 \times 5}$ equal to?

A4 What is the largest amount one can have in standard British coins, yet still not be able to make exactly £1?

A5 Three 'quarter circles' and one 'three-quarter circle' – all of radius 10 cm – make this attractive 'jug' shape. What is its area?

A6 It is a curious fact that the 'false' cancellation shown here gives the right answer. Can you find a similar 'false equation' with the correct value $\frac{2}{5}$ on the right-hand side?

A7 All measurements shown are in centimetres. What is the total area of the shaded region?

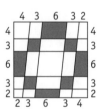

A8 In the game Fizz-Buzz, players take turns to say consecutive whole numbers starting at 1; but in place of each number which contains the digit '5' or which is divisible by 5 one has to say 'Fizz', and in place of each number which contains the digit '7' or which is divisible by 7 one has to say 'Buzz'. How many of the numbers from 1 to 50 do *not* get replaced by 'Fizz' or 'Buzz'?

A9 This solid cube has had its corners cut off to create three new 'corners' at each old 'corner'. If the 24 corners are joined to each other by diagonals, how many of these diagonals lie *completely inside* the 'cube'?

A10 Two candles have different lengths and different thicknesses. The shorter one would last eleven hours, the longer one would last for seven hours. Both candles are lit at the same time, and after three hours both have the same length remaining. What was the ratio of their original lengths?

1995: Section B

B1 Take any two-digit number. Subtract the sum of its digits. Then divide the answer by 9. What do you find? Explain!

B2 The time shown by a digital clock at 21:15 has the curious property that it reads exactly the same after reflection in a vertical mirror. How many such times are there in the course of 24 hours?

B3 Which of the shaded rectangles has the larger area?

B4 Choose any starting number other than 1. To get a new number divide the number that is 1 bigger than your number by the number that is 1 less than your number. Now do the same with this new number. What happens? Explain!

B5 Nine squares are arranged to form a rectangle as shown (not to scale). The smallest square has sides of length 1. How long are the sides of the next smallest square?

B6 I write out the numbers 1, 2, 3, 4 in a circle. Starting at 1, I cross out every second integer till just one number remains: 2 goes first, then 4, leaving 1 and 3; 3 goes next, leaving 1 – so '1' is the last number left. Suppose I start with 1, 2, 3, . . ., n in a circle. For which values of n will the number '1' be the last number left?

1994: Section A

A1 What is the angle between the hands of a clock at 9:30?

A2 For how many two-digit numbers is the sum of the digits a multiple of 6?

A3 While watching their flocks by night the shepherds managed to lose two-thirds of their sheep. They found four-fifths of these again in the morning. What fraction of their original flock did they then have left?

A4 Two cubical dice each have faces numbered 0, 1, 2, 3, 4, 5. When both dice are thrown what is the probability that the total score is a prime number?

A5 *ABCD* is a rectangle with *AB* twice as long as *BC*. *E* is a point such that *ABE* is an equilateral triangle which overlaps the rectangle *ABCD*. *M* is the midpoint of the side *BE*. How big is the angle *CMB*?

A6 A normal duck has two legs. A lame duck has one leg. A sitting duck has no legs. Ninety nine ducks have a total of 100 legs. Given that there are half as many sitting ducks as normal ducks and lame ducks put together, find the number of lame ducks.

A7 How many different solutions are there to this division? (Different letters stand for different digits, and no number begins with zero.)

A8 Moses is twice as old as Methuselah was when Methuselah was one-third as old as Moses will be when Moses is as old as Methuselah is now. If the difference in their ages is 666, how old is Methuselah?

A9 What is the sum of the four angles *a*, *b*, *c*, *d* in the diagram?

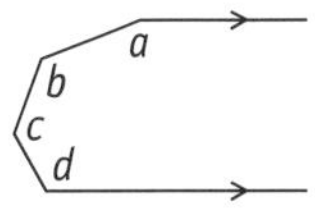

11

A10 A crossnumber is like a crossword except that the answers are numbers, with one digit in each square. What is the sum of all eight digits in this crossnumber?

Across	1.	Square of a prime
	4.	Prime
	5.	Square
Down	1.	Square of another prime
	2.	Square
	3.	Prime

1	2	3
4		
5		■

1994: Section B

B1 A circle of radius 1 is cut into four equal arcs, which are then arranged to make the shape shown here. What is its area? Explain!

B2 (a) Find three prime numbers such that the sum of all three is also a prime.
(b) Find three positive integers such that the sum of any two is a perfect square. Can you find other sets of three integers with the same property?

B3 In the trapezium *PQRS,* angle *QRS* is twice angle *QPS, QR* has length *a* and *RS* has length *b*. What is the length of *PS*? Explain!

B4 A sequence of fractions obeys the following rule: given any two successive terms *a*, *b* of the sequence, the next term is obtained by dividing their product *a.b* by their sum *a* + *b*. If the first two terms are $\frac{1}{2}$ and $\frac{1}{3}$, write down the next three terms. What is the tenth term? Explain clearly what is going on, and how you can be sure.

B5 In this grid, small squares are called *adjacent* if they are next to each other either horizontally or vertically. When you place the digits 1–9 in the nine squares, how many adjacent *pairs* of numbers are there?

You have to arrange the digits 1–9 in the grid so that the total *T* of all the differences between adjacent pairs is as large as possible. Show how this can be done. Explain clearly why no other arrangement could give a larger total *T* than yours.

B6 In the figure described in problem **1994 A5**, what fraction of the rectangle is covered by the equilateral triangle *ABE*?

1993: Section A

A1 Given any number we can multiply the digits together to get another number. We can then do the same to this new number, and repeat again and again until we get down to a single-digit number. If you start with 1993, what single-digit number do you end up with?

A2 A rectangle is cut into four pieces as shown. The areas of three of them are given. What is the total area of the rectangle?

6	10
9	

A3 Write *as a fraction* the answer to the sum on the right (both decimals go on for ever).

$$+ \frac{0.123\,451\,234\,512\,345\,123\ldots}{0.987\,659\,876\,598\,765\,987\ldots}$$

A4 Three ropes of lengths 8 m, 9 m, 10 m are laid on the ground as shown. *AB* is the longest of the three arcs. How long is it?

A5 Two numbers are such that their difference, their sum, and their product are in the ratio 1 : 4 : 15. What are the two numbers?

A6 The radius of the two smallest circles is one-sixth that of the largest circle. The radius of the middle-sized circle is double that of the small circles. What fraction of the large circle is shaded?

A7 A sequence of points in the plane with coordinates (x, y) is determined by the rule that any point with coordinates (x, y) is followed by the point with coordinates $(x + 2y, 2x - y)$. The first point in the sequence is (a, b). What is the fifth point?

A8 *ABCDEFGH* is a 3 by 3 by 3 cube. *X* is one-third of the way along *AB*, *Y* is one-third of the way along *GH*, and *Z* is two-thirds of the way down *DE*. Find the area of triangle *XYZ*.

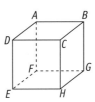

A9 At what time is the angle between the two hands of a clock exactly 170°?

A10 In how many different ways can one pay 20p using standard British coins?

1993: Section B

B1 Place the numbers 1–8 at the vertices of a cube so that the four numbers at the corners of each face always have the same sum. What do you notice about the two numbers at A and B and the two numbers at C and D? Explain clearly why this is not an accident.

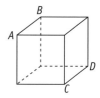

B2 31.3.93 is an 'interesting' date since $31 \times 3 = 93$. If all dates are written like this, how many years of the twentieth century contain no interesting dates at all?

B3 (a) A 2 by 2 square has semicircles drawn on each edge as shown. The overlaps create four shaded 'petals'. Find the shaded area.

(b) A regular *hexagon* with sides of length 2 has semicircles drawn on each side (pointing inwards as before). Find the total area of the six 'petals'.

B4 Does there exist a four-digit number '*aabb*' which is a perfect square and whose first two digits are the same and whose last two digits are the same?

B5 Everyone knows that $2 + 2 = 2 \times 2$. Which other pairs of numbers a, b satisfy $a + b = a \times b$? Can you find three numbers a, b, c such that $a + b + c = a.b.c$? How about four numbers a, b, c, d such that $a + b + c + d = a.b.c.d$? How about five? Six? ...

B6 *ABCD* is a square with centre O. A' is the midpoint of AO, and B', C', D' are the midpoints of BO, CO, DO respectively. The two parallelograms $AB'CD'$ and $A'BC'D$ overlap. How big is this overlap as a fraction of the square $ABCD$?

1992: Section A

A1 Which multiple of 11 is nearest to 1000?

A2 This cuboid has volume $\frac{1}{4}$ cm³.
What is its width?

A3 $8 = 3 + 5$ is the sum of two different prime numbers. What is the smallest whole number which can be written as the sum of two different prime numbers in two different ways?

A4 On holiday I always wear pants, shorts, T-shirt and sunglasses. I have to put on the T-shirt before the sunglasses, and the pants before the shorts. Each day I dress in a different order. For how long can I keep this up?

A5 The first term of a sequence is $\frac{3}{8}$. Each new term is obtained by working out $\frac{(1-x)}{(1+x)}$ where x is the previous term. What is the eighth term?

A6 Four pipes each of diameter 1 m are held tightly together by a metal band as shown. How long is the band?

A7 In question **A6** what is the cross-sectional area of the hole in the middle?

A8 My children are all at school. The product of their ages is 60 060. How many children have I got?

A9 The Earth has radius 6500 km, and rotates on its axis once every 24 hours. If I stand with one foot either side of the Equator, at what approximate speed (in km/h) would the Earth be whizzing me round?

A10 The date 29.2.92 is interesting: it is a *palindromic* date because it reads the same both forwards and backwards. How many palindromic dates are there between 1910 and 1999?

17

1992: Section B

B1 Does there exist a two-digit number '*ab*' such that the difference between '*ab*' and its reverse '*ba*' is a prime number?

B2 A*BCDEFGH* is a regular octagon (eight sides). How big is angle *ADG*?

B3 If x is any non-zero number, then $\frac{1}{x}$ is called the *inverse* of x. A sequence of numbers begins 1,1, ... From then on each new term is obtained by adding the inverses of the two previous terms and then taking the inverse of the answer. So to get the third term we add $\frac{1}{1}$ and $\frac{1}{1}$ to get 2, and the third term is then the inverse of this answer, namely $\frac{1}{2}$. Find the eighth term, and explain (with proof) how the sequence continues.

B4 What is the surface area of a cube which just fits inside a sphere of radius 1 cm?

B5 (a) Which primes can be expressed as the difference of two squares?
    (b) Which primes can be expressed as the difference of two squares in two (or more) different ways?

B6 Find the area of the shaded region in the diagram.

1991: Section A

A1 What is the largest prime factor of 1991?

A2 Ann and Ben work as a team. How long must they work to earn £66 if Ann is paid £$\frac{5}{6}$ for each $\frac{4}{5}$ hours she works and Ben is paid £$\frac{7}{8}$ for each $\frac{6}{7}$ hours?

A3 $ABCD$ is a square. M is the midpoint of BC and N is the midpoint of AD. The circle through M with centre N cuts CD at P. How big is the angle PNM?

A4 Find a number less than 100 which is increased by 20% when its digits are reversed.

A5 The boundary of the curved shape on the right consists of six semicircles, each of radius 1 cm. The centres of the six circles used form the vertices of a regular hexagon. Find the area enclosed by the curve (in square centimetres).

A6 Razia broke her necklace. She found one-third of the beads on the floor, one-quarter in her pocket, one-fifth down the side of the sofa, while one-sixth remained on the string; six beads were never found. How many beads were there to start with?

A7 A circular clock has twelve dots round its rim at the hour marks. The dots at 12, 2, 3, 6, 8, 9 are denoted by A, B, C, D, E, F respectively. Find the ratio of the areas of the two quadrilaterals $ABDE$ and $ACDF$.

A8 The first two terms of a sequence are a and b. Each new term is obtained by dividing the previous term by the one before that. What is the eighth term in the sequence?

A9 A net for a pyramid has a square base of side length 10 cm with an equilateral triangle on each side of the square. What will be the height of the pyramid after it has been made?

A10 In how many ways can 105 be written as the sum of two or more consecutive positive integers?

1991: Section B

B1 1991 is a *palindrome*: it reads the same both forwards and backwards. How long before 1991 was the previous palindromic year? What are the shortest and the longest possible gaps between one palindromic year and the next?

B2 The year 1991 uses just two different digits. How many years since AD 1 (up to 1991) used just two different digits?

B3 (a) Write the perfect square 9 as the sum of two perfect cubes. What is the next perfect square which is equal to the sum of two different cubes?
(b) Can a perfect square ever be written as the sum of three squares?

B4 For which positive integers N is it possible to construct a polygon with N sides all the same length and such that any two successive sides are at right angles? Prove your assertion.

B5 Two walls, one of height a metres and the other of height b metres, are d metres apart. A ladder of length l metres has its feet hinged at a point between the two walls and can just reach the top of each. The two positions of the ladder are at right angles. How many different solutions are there for a, b, d, l if all four have to be positive integers less than 20?

B6 Eebs have honeycombs with *square* cells, all packed tightly together. An eeb grub starts in one cell. Each day it moves to a neighbouring cell, possibly revisiting a cell it occupied on a previous occasion.

(a) Suppose it starts in a cell *in the middle* of the honeycomb. How many different cells would you have to look in to be sure of finding it on the nth day?

(b) What if the grub starts *in a corner cell* as shown here? How many different cells would you have to look in to be sure of finding it on the nth day?

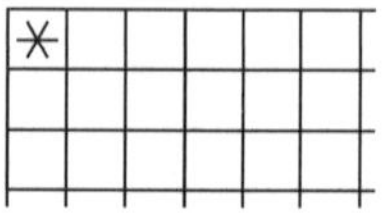

1990: Section A

A1 1990 is exactly ten times a prime number. When is the next year after 1990 which is exactly ten times a prime number?

A2 A sheet of card measuring 30 cm by 21 cm is to be cut up to make as many tickets as possible, each one measuring 6 cm by 8 cm. How many tickets can be made?

A3 How many primes less than 10 000 have digits adding up to 2?

A4 The corners of a regular hexagon (in order) are P, Q, R, S, T, U. PT and SU cross at the point V. How big is the angle TVS?

A5 The digit 3 is written at the right of a certain two-digit number to make a three-digit number. The new number is 777 more than the original two-digit number. What was the original number?

A6 An equilateral triangle and a regular hexagon have equal perimeters. What is the ratio of the area of the triangle to the area of the hexagon?

A7 A school running track has six lanes, each 1 metre wide. How far forward should the runner in the outside lane start if a one-lap race is to be fair?

A8 The sun is $60°$ above the horizon. A vertical tree, 60 ft high, casts its shadow straight down a $30°$ slope. How long is the shadow?

A9 A new operation $\star$ for combining two numbers a and b is defined by

$$a \star b = \frac{(a+b)}{2}$$

If $x \star (x \star 14) = x$, what is x?

A10 London has longitude $0°$. Cardiff has the same latitude as London but has longitude $3°$ W. On Midsummer's Day the sun rises in London at 4:43am BST (British Summer Time). At what time does the sun rise in Cardiff on that day?

1990: Section B

B1 In how many ways can the word 'MATHS' be traced out in this diagram if you are only allowed to move one step at a time horizontally or vertically, up or down, backwards or forwards?

```
          S
        S H S
      S H T H S
    S H T A T H S
  S H T A M A T H S
    S H T A T H S
      S H T H S
        S H S
          S
```

B2 A man goes to the bank to draw x pounds and y pence. Instead he is given y pounds and x pence. After spending one pound he still has twice as much as the bank should have given him in the first place. How much did he intend to draw?

B3 In Lower Polygonia the unit of currency is the **gon**. Only three kinds of coins are in circulation: 5 gons, 9 gons and 12 gons. What amounts of money cannot be made up exactly by a suitable combination of these coins?

B4 A cylindrical barrel of diameter 1 metre lies on its side right up against a wall. My ball just fits in the gap between the barrel, the floor, and the wall. How big is my ball?

B5 (a) Notice that $9 = 3^2$ is very nearly the average of two other squares. What are they?

(b) Find three squares for which the middle one is *exactly* the average of the other two.

(c) Find three more squares for which the middle one is exactly the average of the other two. Show that there are infinitely many such triples.

B6 In ordinary 3 by 3 noughts and crosses there are eight winning lines: three horizontal, three vertical and two diagonal.

(a) How many winning lines (three-in-a-row) are there in 4 by 4 noughts and crosses? How many are there in n by n noughts and crosses?

(b) How many winning lines (three-in-a-row) are there in three-dimensional 3 by 3 by 3 noughts and crosses? How many in 4 by 4 by 4 noughts and crosses? How many in n by n by n noughts and crosses?

1989

The first UK JMO was very much an experiment. No one had any idea what kind of 'Olympiad-type' questions one could ask UK pupils of this age. We also had no experience of how to structure a paper so that students would benefit from the experience of struggling to solve hard problems. We deliberately aimed high to get some idea 'where to draw the line' for future years. Thus this paper is untypical, in that (in the language of the 1990–95 papers) it consists of 'one very long Section B', from which it was hoped that serious candidates would solve (say) three or more problems. The questions are nevertheless in a similar style, and are included in this collection in the hope that they will still be of interest.

1 Find the smallest multiple of 9 which has no odd digits.

2 The two small semicircles inside the big circle divide the big circle into two congruent pieces. Explain how to cut both the shaded and unshaded regions exactly in half with a single straight cut.

3 Describe how you could multiply 7 628 954 301 by 125 in your head.

4 Joining each vertex in the big regular hexagon to the next vertex but one produces a smaller hexagon inside. Prove that the smaller hexagon is regular. Find its edge length in terms of the edge length of the big hexagon.

5 Find two perfect squares that differ by 105. How many different solutions are there?

6 A right-angled triangle has legs of length a and b. A circle of radius r touches the two legs and has its centre on the hypotenuse. Show that

$$\frac{1}{a} + \frac{1}{b} + \frac{1}{r}$$

7 Find all ordered pairs of numbers (x, y) whose sum $x + y$, product $x.y$, and quotient $\frac{x}{y}$ are all equal.

8 The diagram shows an equilateral triangle with sides of length 3 cut into nine equilateral triangles of side length 1. Place the numbers 1 to 9 in the nine small triangles so that the sum of the numbers inside any equilateral triangle with side length 2 is the same. What are the smallest and largest possible values of this sum?

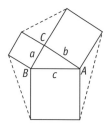

9 The three sides a, b, c of a triangle are such that $a^2 + b^2 + c^2 = ab + bc + ca$. Does the triangle have to be equilateral?

10 Pythagoras' theorem for the right-angled triangle ABC is often illustrated by a diagram like the one shown here (without the dotted lines). Putting in the three dotted lines shows that the whole figure can be enclosed in a hexagon. Find the area of this hexagon in terms of the edge lengths a, b, c of the original triangle.

11 (a) $5^2 = 4^2 + 3^2$. If we ignore multiples of this equation (such as $10^2 = 8^2 + 6^2$), what is the next square which can be written as the sum of two squares?

(b) $6^3 = 5^3 + 4^3 + 3^3$. If we ignore multiples of this equation (such as $12^3 = 10^3 + 8^3 + 6^3$), what is the next cube which can be written as the sum of three cubes?

12 Two straight cuts, one through each of two vertices of a triangle, divide the triangle into three smaller triangles and one quadrilateral.

(a) Is it possible for the areas of all four parts to be equal?

(b) More generally, if three of the parts have area p while the fourth has area q, what are the possible values of $\frac{p}{q}$?

13 Mr and Mrs *A* invite some other married couples to dinner. As they all meet, some pairs shake hands. Married couples do not shake hands with one another. Over coffee, while Mr *A* is washing up, the rest discover that they all shook hands a different number of times.

(a) Suppose there were four couples altogether (including Mr and Mrs *A*). Can you say how many hands Mr *A* must have shaken?

(b) What if there were five couples altogether? Can you say how many hands Mr *A* must have shaken?

Sixty additional problems

Section A problems

Solutions to Section A problems should consist of a clearly presented, exact calculation, leading to a numerical answer. Do not use a calculator.

1 If Gilda had subtracted her two numbers as she was meant to, she would have got the answer 2. Instead she divided the two numbers and got the answer $2.\dot{2}$. What were her two starting numbers?

2 When a barrel is 30% empty it contains 30 gallons more than when it is 30% full. How many gallons does the barrel hold when full?

3 What is 30% of 40% of 50?

4 A square peg just fits inside a round hole. What fraction of the hole is occupied by the peg?

5 Evaluate $\left[\left(\frac{1}{2} + \frac{1}{3}\right) \div \frac{1}{4}\right] \times \frac{1}{5} - \frac{1}{6}$.

6 If four mice can eat four pounds of cheese in four minutes, how long will it take 99 mice to eat 99 pounds of cheese?

7 In a regular octagon, what is the ratio of the length of its longest diagonal to the length of its shortest diagonal?

8 Basil was meant to take the fourth root of a number, but instead divided by four and got the answer 4. What should his answer have been?

9 Evaluate $12\,345\,679 \times 9$.

10 One-half of the class got As. One-third of the rest got Bs. One-quarter of the remainder got Cs. One-fifth of the others got Ds. What fraction of the class got Es or worse?

11 Precisely one of the numbers

$$234, \quad 2345, \quad 23\,456, \quad 234\,567, \quad 2\,345\,678, \quad 23\,456\,789$$

is a prime number. Which one must it be?

12 A paper cylinder of radius r (without a top or a bottom) has the same surface area as a sphere of radius r. What is the height of the cylinder?

13 A two-digit number is such that, if a decimal point is placed between its two digits, the resulting number is one-quarter of the sum of the two digits. What is the original number?

14 One millionth of a second is a *microsecond*. Roughly how long is a *microcentury*?

15 Thirty-eight children are seated, equally spaced, around a circle. They are numbered in order from 1 up to 38. What is the number of the child opposite child number 8?

16 How many prime numbers between 10 and 99 remain prime when the order of their two digits is reversed?

17 Start with a circular disc of radius r. Two further circles, of radius a and radius b respectively, fit tightly inside the circle of radius r. What is the perimeter of the upper shaded region?

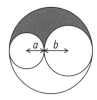

18 What is 10% of 20 plus 20% of 30 plus 30% of 40 take away 50% of 60?

19 Evaluate $1 + 22 + 333 + 4444 + 55\,555 + 666\,666 + 7\,777\,777 + 88\,888\,888 + 999\,999\,999$.

20 Given a cube, each set of four vertices A, B, C, D in the same plane produces a quadrilateral. How many of these quadrilaterals are *rectangles*?

21 I travel 9 miles east, then 20 miles north, then 30 miles west. How far am I then from my starting point?

22 Find the exact value of $(666\,666\,666)^2 - (333\,333\,333)^2$.

23 Two cylindrical candles – one of diameter 1 cm and height 1 cm and one of diameter 2 cm and height 2 cm – are melted down to make a cylindrical candle of diameter 3 cm. What will its height be?

24 A giant tortoise is being transported by train across the Nullarbor Plain in Western Australia – one of the longest straight pieces of railway track in the world. On the tortoise's back is a hairy caterpillar, and on the caterpillar's back is a flea. In the time it takes the train to travel 10 km forwards, the tortoise crawls 10 m backwards, the caterpillar wriggles 10 cm forwards and the flea jumps 10 mm backwards. How far overall has the flea travelled forwards in this time?

25 PQR is a triangle and S is a point on PR such that $QS = PS = RS$. If QS divides the angle PQR in the ratio $5 : 4$, how big is the larger of the two angles at Q?

26 How many times each day do the hands of a clock point in exactly opposite directions?

27 A British 50p coin is not circular, but has constant diameter D. What is its perimeter?

28 x men work x hours a day for x days to dig an x km length of tunnel. If y men work y hours a day for y days on the same tunnel, what length of tunnel would you expect them to dig?

29 An aeroplane propeller of radius 1 m moves so that the tip of the propeller goes round exactly once in the time it takes the plane to move forward 1 m. How far does the tip of each propeller blade move during one such rotation?

30 How many whole numbers less than 100 can be written as the product of two even numbers?

31 Three discs of radius 1 fit snugly together without overlapping, but with each one touching the other two. What is the area of the 'curvy triangle' in the middle?

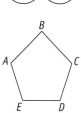

32 The pentagon *ABCDE* has a right angle at *B*, $AB = BC$, and $CD = DE = EA = 1$, $AC = 2$. If *AC* and *ED* are parallel, find the area of the pentagon.

33 A sequence of terms, chosen from {1, 2, 3, 4, 5, 6, 7, 8}, is such that the second term is bigger than the first, and each term after the first two is greater than the sum of the previous two terms. If the sequence has just one or two terms this is no restriction at all! How many possible sequences of this kind are there with at least three terms?

34 What fraction of this regular octagon is shaded?

35 You are given a circle of radius *r*. Let *s* be the area of the square inscribed in the upper semicircle, and *c* the area of the square inscribed in the circle.

Find $\frac{c}{s}$.

36 To get to school from home I have to cycle one mile up a hill and one mile down the other side. If I average 10 miles per hour (mph) on the way up, what speed must I go down the other side if I am to average 20 mph for the whole journey?

37 A sphere just fits inside a cube, and the cube just fits inside a cylinder (touching the sides and both the top and the bottom faces). What fraction of the cylinder is occupied by the sphere?

38 Given a cube, each selection of three vertices *A*, *B*, *C* produces a triangle. How many of these triangles are *right-angled* triangles?

39 These numbers are 'pumpwarts':

16 325, 34 721, 12 347, 52 163, 90 341, 50 381.

These numbers are *not* 'pumpwarts':

2564, 12 345, 854, 12 635, 34 325, 45 026.

Which of the following numbers is a 'pumpwart'?

72 521, 72 341, 4562, 13 562, 38 521.

40 Calculate (exactly!) the shaded area in the diagram.

Section B problems

Section B problems usually involve a degree of exploration. Your final solution may be quite short, but must be presented logically, with clear explanations and proofs. Answers should be exact, and in fully simplified form. Do not use a calculator.

1 I take a (secret) two-digit number; double it; multiply the answer by five; subtract the number I started with; divide the answer by nine; then subtract the number I started with. What are the possible final answers? Explain!

2 *ABCD* is a square, *M* is the midpoint of *AB* and *N* is the midpoint of *DA*. The lines *CM* and *BN* cross at *Y*. How big is the angle *CYN*? Explain!

3 (a) How many different three-digit numbers can one make using the digits 1, 3, 7 once each? How many of these numbers are prime numbers?
  (b) For which three starting digits does one get the largest number of prime numbers in this way?

4 (a) In a 4 by 4 grid there are exactly 25 'grid points'. How many different distances are there between pairs of distinct grid points? Explain.
  (b) How many different distances are there between pairs of distinct grid points in a 5 by 5 grid? A 6 by 6 grid? A 7 by 7 grid? Explain.

5 The diagram shows a rectangular piece of paper with a circular hole cut out of it. Explain how to cut the remaining paper exactly in half with a single straight cut.

31

6 (a) Choose any number between 3 and 27. Multiply your number by 37. Form a new number by shifting the left-hand digit to the right-hand end. Divide your new number by 37. What happens? Does it always work? Explain.

(b) Choose any number between 244 and 2439. Multiply your number by 41. Form a new number by shifting the left-hand digit to the right-hand end. Divide your new number by 41. What happens? Does it always work? Explain.

7 A circular clockface with centre C has twelve hour marks. The one o'clock and two o'clock hour marks are O and T respectively. The circle centre O through T cuts CT again at D. Where does OD cut the circumference of the clockface? Explain!

8 (a) I have lots of 1p and 2p stamps. In how many different ways can I make up 8p? In how many ways can I make up 80p?

(b) I have lots of 1p, 2p and 3p stamps. In how many different ways can I make up 8p? In how many ways can I make up 80p?

9 (a) $\frac{1}{2}$ and $\frac{1}{4}$ both have decimals that terminate. Find an integer $n \geq 3$ such that $\frac{1}{n}$ and $\frac{1}{(n+2)}$ both have decimals that terminate.

(b) $\frac{1}{5}$ and $\frac{1}{8}$ both have decimals that terminate. Find an integer $n \geq 6$ such that $\frac{1}{n}$ and $\frac{1}{(n+3)}$ both have decimals that terminate.

(c) Are there any other pairs $(n, n + 2)$ as in (a), or $(n, n + 3)$ as in (b) with $n < 1000$? Explain!

10 (a) Is it possible to cover a 5 by 5 square with non-overlapping 3 by 1 rectangles? Explain.

(b) Is it possible to cover a 6 by 6 square with T-shaped pieces of the kind shown here? Explain.

11 Take two positive numbers. Divide the first by the second, then divide the second by the first, then subtract the two answers; finally multiply by the product of the two original numbers, and divide the answer by the difference of the two original numbers. What do you get? Explain!

12 In an unknown triangle *ABC*, *M* is the midpoint of *CA* and *N* is the midpoint of *AB*. The lines *BM* and *CN* cross at the point *G*.
   (a) Prove that triangles *BGN* and *CGM* have equal areas.
   (b) Prove that the area of triangle *BGC* is one-third of the area of triangle *ABC*.

13 (a) Given any two-digit number *N*, multiply the digits together to get a new number. Do the same to the new number, repeating until you end with a single-digit answer. If you work through all the numbers in the 20s, how many different final answers are possible? Which run of ten (the 10s, 20s, 30s, 40s, 50s, 60s, 70s, 80s or 90s) produces the fewest final answers?
   (b) Extend this idea to numbers with more than two digits. Among all possible runs of ten numbers (for example, from 1760 to 1769), what is the smallest possible number of final answers?

14 A 2 by 8 rectangle can be cut up and rearranged to make a 4 by 4 square. However, the starting rectangle has shortest side only a quarter as long as the longest side.
   (a) Find a rectangle, which can be cut up and rearranged to make a square, in which the shortest side is more than half as long as the longest side.
   (b) Find a rectangle, which can be cut up and rearranged to make a square, in which the shortest side is more than two-thirds as long as the longest side.
   (c) Find a rectangle, which can be cut up and rearranged to make a square, in which the shortest side is more than three-quarters as long as the longest side.

15 *N* is a positive integer and $N^2 - 2000$ is a perfect square. How many possible values are there for *N*? Explain.

16 *ABCDEF* is a regular hexagon of side 2. *M* is the midpoint of *CD*.
   (a) Calculate the length of *AM*.
   (b) If *N* is the midpoint of *EF*, and *AM*, *BN* cross at the point *X*, find angle *AXB*.

17 How many non-overlapping discs of radius 1 can one fit inside an 8 by 8 square? How many such discs can one fit inside a 9 by 9 square? How many will fit in a 100 by 100 square?

18 How many ways are there of paying 50p using standard British coins (1p, 2p, 5p, 10p, 20p, 50p)? How many ways are there of paying £1?

19 A bug travels from S to F on the outside of this 'Rubik's cube', keeping to the grid lines.
How long is each shortest route from S to F?
How many different 'shortest routes' are there from S to F?

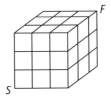

20 (a) In how many different ways can one put six milk bottles in a 3 by 3 crate so that there are exactly two bottles in each row and two in each column?
(b) In how many different ways can one put ten milk bottles in a 5 by 5 crate so that there are exactly two bottles in each row and each column?

Comments and hints

It is not easy to convey the intended spirit of each paper. Section A problems are meant to be a challenging way of 'warming up'. The really important part is Section B. In Section B exploration may be important, but it is important as a precursor to writing a genuinely mathematical solution. 'To solve a problem' it is *not* sufficient to give a formally correct answer.

> When we ask 'What is the smallest angle whose sine is equal to $\frac{1}{2}$?', we are not interested in the response 'sin$^{-1}(\frac{1}{2})$'!

To solve a problem completely means to discover, and explain mathematically, a way of looking at the problem which makes it transparent, and which produces the most meaningful answer – that is, an answer which is not only correct, but which is as simple and as enlightening as possible.

Such ideas are important, accessible, and highly satisfying to students of all ages. It is also important that the associated insight into what mathematics is really about – and in particular that it is *not* about mere 'pattern-spotting' – must be understood *early*.

This section contains brief comments on almost every problem. The comments are of two kinds. Some of the comments focus on common errors which occurred in candidates' attempted solutions in the relevant UK JMO. Other comments are more in the way of encouragement to the problem solver, providing a hint of some kind without revealing too much of the final solution. If you get stuck on a problem, the comments and hints in this section should be consulted *before* looking at the *Outline solutions*.

> Make sure you have a go at each problem as you work through these comments.

1995: Section A

A1 Evaluate 123 123 ÷ 1001.

No one should get this wrong (though lots did). The simplest way is probably to use long division; but you may prefer to think of 123 123 as 'so many thousands and so many units'.

A2 **What is the size of the angle x?**

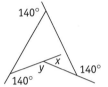

Mathematical problems have to be solved by *exact* calculation. Far too many candidates *assumed* that the angle y must be equal to 140°.

A3 What is $\dfrac{1}{1 \times 2} + \dfrac{1}{2 \times 3} + \dfrac{1}{3 \times 4} + \dfrac{1}{4 \times 5}$ equal to?

The simplest approach is to rewrite each of the four fractions using a common denominator. After adding the four bits together, remember to simplify your answer!

A4 **What is the largest amount one can have in standard British coins (1p, 2p, 5p, 20p, 50p, £1 = 100p), yet still not be able to make exactly £1?**

The answer is bigger than you might expect. (In particular, it is much more than 99p!) Once you realise this, it should not be too hard to find what you *think* is the answer. The challenge is to explain correctly why your answer is right!

A5 **Three 'quarter circles' and one 'three-quarter circle' (all of radius 10 cm) make this jug shape. What is its area?**

It is no use measuring, or guessing. All those bumps and dents should suggest the idea of cutting the shape into pieces and rearranging them to form some very simple shape. Start by marking the centres of the four circles used to make the shape!

A6 'Cancelling the two 9s' in $\frac{19}{95}$ is wrong, but gives the correct answer $\frac{1}{5}$. Can you find a similar 'false equation' with the correct value $\frac{2}{5}$ on the right-hand side?

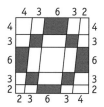

You need some fraction of the form 'twenty-*ump* over *umpty*-five'. It then comes down to how well you know your tables. Learning to juggle numbers in your head is an important skill.

A7 All measurements shown are in centimetres. What is the total area of the shaded region?

Areas have to be calculated exactly.
You must not guess, or estimate.

A8 How many numbers from 1 to 50 are divisible by neither 5 nor 7, and have neither 5 nor 7 as a digit?

One way to get an answer is to write out all the numbers from 1 to 50; then cross off all those which are divisible by 5 or 7, or which have 5 or 7 as a digit; finally count how many numbers are left. This might work; but it is a lousy method, for you would never know whether you had made a mistake. For counting to be *mathematical* (and hence reliable), it must be carefully *structured*. Try to devise a method that would work almost as quickly for the numbers 1–100, or 1–500.

A9 This solid cube has had its corners cut off to create three new 'corners' at each old 'corner'. If the 24 corners are joined to each other by diagonals, how many of these diagonals lie *completely inside* the 'cube'?

This is not at all easy. The comment on question **A8** above applies even more emphatically here: for counting to be mathematical, it must be carefully *structured*. So think carefully before you start counting.

A10 Two candles have different lengths and different thicknesses. The shorter one would last eleven hours, the longer one would last for seven hours. Both candles are lit at the same time, and after three hours both have the same length remaining. What was the ratio of their original lengths?

Somehow you have to set up an *equation* which compares the lengths of the two candles. You are told that 'after three hours, both have the same length remaining'. What fraction of the shorter candle is left after three hours? And what fraction of the longer candle is left?

1995: Section B

B1 Take any two-digit number. Subtract the sum of its digits. Then divide the answer by 9. What do you find? Explain!

The question 'What do you find?' suggests that something slightly unexpected happens, no matter what two-digit number you start with. Your first task is to state as clearly as you can *what* happens. Your second task is to *prove* that what you think happens really does always happen. For this it is not enough to check a few cases: you must find a completely general argument.

B2 The time shown by a digital clock at 21:15 has the curious property that it reads exactly the same after reflection in a vertical mirror. How many such times are there in the course of 24 hours?

There is more than one way of going at this. But, whichever approach you use, it is not enough just to state 'There are _____ times', or even to write out a list of times which work. You have to explain clearly, and as simply as you can, *why your list is complete*. Mathematics is 'the art of reasoning correctly'.

B3 Which of the shaded rectangles has the larger area?

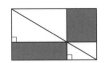

Diagrams in mathematics are never drawn 'to scale'.

The question refers to a rectangle, without giving its size. Nor does it say how far up the diagonal the two extra lines cross. Your solution must therefore work for all possible sizes of rectangle and all possible positions of the two extra lines.

B4 Choose any starting number other than 1. To get a new number divide the number that is 1 bigger than your number by the number that is 1 less than your number. Now do the same with this new number. What happens? Explain!

If you choose a particular starting number and follow these instructions, then, provided your arithmetic is reliable, you should soon discover something interesting. That is where the mathematics *begins*! You must then *prove* that what you suspect happens, really does always happen. For that you will need to use a∗∗e∗∗a.

B5 Nine squares are arranged to form a rectangle as shown (not to scale). The smallest square has sides of length 1. How long are the sides of the next smallest square?

You cannot conclude anything by measuring on the diagram; diagrams in mathematics are never drawn exactly to scale. However, you can tell from the diagram which of the two squares *A* and *B* is bigger (Why?) and which of the two squares *B* and *C* is bigger. If you carry on in this way, you can tell which square is the 'second smallest'. Then all you need is some way of calculating its size *exactly*.

B6 I write out the numbers 1, 2, 3, 4 in a circle. Starting at 1, I cross out every second integer till just one number remains: 2 goes first, then 4, leaving 1 and 3; 3 goes next, leaving 1. Suppose I start with 1, 2, 3, . . ., *n* in a circle. For which values of *n* will the number '1' be the last number left?

The question 'For which values of *n* . . .?' is more complicated than it looks. It is not enough to answer '*n* = 4' (even though *n* = 4 works), since we clearly want to know *all* possible values of *n* that work. Hence a solution must not only show that certain values of *n* work, but must also somehow prove that *no other values of n could possibly work*.

1994: Section A

A1 What is the angle between the hands of a clock at 9:30?

If you are in any doubt you *must* draw a diagram. You should know where the minute hand is (exactly!) at 9:30. And you should know that the hour hand is *not* pointing at the 9!

A2 **For how many two-digit numbers is the sum of the digits a multiple of 6?**

If the sum of the digits is a multiple of 6, it must be either 6, or _____, or . . . .

A3 **Some shepherds lose two-thirds of their flock and then find four-fifths of these. What fraction of the flock did they have left?**

If 'four-fifths' were found, then 'one-fifth' remained lost. But think carefully: one-fifth of what?

A4 **Two dice labelled 0–5 are thrown. Find the probability that the total is a prime number.**

Think of the two dice as having different colours – say red and blue. The blue dice can show any one of six numbers, as can the red dice. This should tell you exactly how many different 'blue–red combinations' are possible – say N. Each of these combinations has the same probability $\frac{1}{N}$, you only have to count the number of different blue–red combinations that give a prime total.

(**Note:** 0 and 1 are not prime numbers. 0 is certainly not prime, since every number is a factor of 0. It is less clear why 1 is not a prime number. Roughly speaking, prime numbers are important because they allow us to factorise large numbers into *smaller* prime factors (for example, $91 = 13 \times 7$); if we factorise using 1s ($91 = 91 \times 1 \times 1 = 13 \times 7 \times 1 \times 1 \times 1 \times \ldots$), the 1s just get in the way. Hence we do not count 1 as a prime number.)

A5 **In the rectangle $ABCD$, $AB = 2 \times BC$; the point E is such that triangle ABE overlaps the rectangle and is equilateral; M is the midpoint of BE. Find $\angle CMB$.**

Part of the problem here is to translate information given *in words* into a (correct) *diagram*. So read the question carefully. Then produce your own diagram. Finally read the question again to check that your diagram is correct.

A6 **A normal duck has two legs. A lame duck has one leg. A sitting duck has no legs. Ninety nine ducks have a total of 100 legs. Given that there are half as many sitting ducks as normal ducks and lame ducks put together, find the number of lame ducks.**

The idea here comes from the Australian Mathematics Competition 1990. I still smile every time I read it! To solve the problem you really have no alternative but to translate the given information into the form of *equations* linking three unknowns: N (the number of normal ducks), L (the number of lame ducks) and S (the number of sitting ducks).

A7 How many different solutions are there to JMO ÷ UK = OK? (Different letters stand for different digits, and no number begins with a zero.)

Every subtraction problem (for example, '135 – 49 =?') is equivalent to an a∗∗i∗io∗ problem ('What must I *add* to 49 to get 135?'). Similarly every division problem is equivalent to a ∗u∗∗i∗∗i∗a∗io∗ problem. Question **A7** only becomes manageable if you make this switch. Even then it is not easy!

A8 Moses is twice as old as Methuselah was when Methuselah was one-third as old as Moses will be when Moses is as old as Methuselah is now. If the difference in their ages is 666, how old is Methuselah?

The key is to read the first sentence of the original problem carefully and to think what it is really saying.

A9 What is the sum of the four angles *a, b, c, d* in the diagram?

The only information about how the diagram is constructed is the two 'arrows' which indicate that the top and bottom lines are ∗a∗a∗∗e∗. So presumably the answer is supposed to be the same whenever two parallel lines are joined by three line segments to create four angles *a, b, c, d*. However, that does *not* mean that you can simply use a protractor. In mathematics measuring on a diagram is never acceptable: one must use *mathematical reasoning* and *exact calculation*.

A10 A crossnumber is like a crossword except that the answers are numbers, with one digit in each square. What is the sum of all eight digits in this crossnumber?

Across	1.	Square of a prime
	4.	Prime
	5.	Square
Down	1.	Square of another prime
	2.	Square
	3.	Prime

1	2	3
4		
5		■

This problem should be treated as a Section B question in that you should keep a careful record of your *reasoning*. By chance the second easiest guesses for *1 Across* and for *1 Down* happen to work. But how can you be sure that there are no other solutions?

1994: Section B

B1 Four quarters of a circle of radius 1 are arranged as shown. Find the area.

The four arcs have the same total *length* as before.

But this is a question about *area*, not about length. The area of the new shape is definitely *not* the same as the area of the original circle. (It was quite shocking how many candidates ignored the evidence of their own eyes and asserted that, if the perimeter is unchanged, then the area must stay the same too.)

B2 **(b)** Find three positive integers such that the sum of any two is a square.

Here 'the sum of any two' really means 'the sum of *each* pair'. If you have three numbers a, b, c, there are three pairs: a, b and b, c and c, a. You have to make sure that each of the sums $a + b$, $b + c$, $c + a$ is a perfect square.

B3 Find the length of *PS*. Explain!

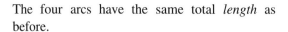

The only lengths given in the figure are a and b. So presumably the length of *PS* only depends on a and b. But it is no good just guessing, or measuring: you have to prove that the length of *PS* is what you claim it is.

In geometry problems you should never expect to answer the question directly from the given diagram. You must be prepared to add one or two carefully chosen lines which help you see what exactly is going on. For example, suppose we drop perpendiculars *QX* and *RY* from *Q* and *R* to *PS*; then *QRYX* is a *e**a***e, so we know that $XY = QR = a$. This shows that part of *PS* has length a, so all that remains is to work out the length of $PX + YS$. Unfortunately this isn't very easy. (Why not? Because the lines *QX* and *RY* we drew in did not make use of the given information about the two angles *QPS* and *QRS*.) Go back to the original diagram. Can you find a single additional line that makes use of *all* the given information and helps solve the problem?

B4 A sequence begins $\frac{1}{2}$, $\frac{1}{3}$. **Given any successive terms a, b, the next term is obtained by dividing their product $a.b$ by their sum $a + b$. Write down the next three terms. Find the tenth term. Explain!**

The key word comes at the very end. Explain! As you work out the third, fourth and fifth terms, you must

(a) work carefully (and simplify each answer as much as possible to avoid getting in a mess at the next stage), and

(b) keep your wits about you to see if you can *guess* what seems to be happening.

But a guess is only the beginning. You must then *prove* that your guess is in fact correct.

B5 **Arrange the numbers 1–9 in a 3 by 3 grid so that the total T of all the horizontal and vertical differences between adjacent squares is as large as possible. Prove that no other arrangement could give a larger total T.**

There are exactly twelve adjacent *pairs* of numbers – corresponding to the twelve internal lines. It is the differences between these twelve pairs that you have to control. This is by far the hardest problem on the 1994 paper. Don't underestimate it. The first four sentences only introduce the problem. The sting is in the final sentence. There are 362 880 different ways to arrange the digits 1–9 in the grid! You are clearly not meant to check them all. But you must not ignore them either. Somehow you have to find what you *believe* to be the best arrangement, and then *prove* that your arrangement *must be better than all the others*.

To find a good arrangement with what looks like a large total T you are free to use anything that seems like a good idea: for example, 'Put a small number in the middle with big numbers round it to get big differences' is a lovely idea which will certainly give a bigger total T than many other arrangements. But how do you know it will give a bigger total T than *all* other arrangements? It might; but you have to explain *why*. Do not underestimate the difficulty of proving that no other way could give a larger total.

B6 Find the fraction of the rectangle *ABCD* in problem 1994 A5 that is covered by triangle *ABE*.

Mathematics must always be based on *exact calculation*, not guesswork (or measuring).

Let *AE* cut *CD* at *X* and *BE* cut *CD* at *Y*. If we drop perpendiculars *XP* and *YQ* from *X* and *Y* to *AB*, then the rectangle *ABCD* is cut into three smaller rectangles *ADXP*, *XYQP*, *BQYC*. All three rectangles certainly have the same height, but one cannot assume they have equal widths. There is in fact a very good *reason* why two of them are equal – and you should give that reason as clearly as you can. But there is no obvious reason why the other rectangle should be the same. It *might* be; but if it is, it would be a great surprise. So you must be willing to do some exact calculations to see.

1993: Section A

A2 Given the areas of the three small rectangles, find the area of the big rectangle.

6	10
9	

Many candidates calculated correctly, but failed to read the question. (The answer is not 15!)

A3 Find $0.123\,451\,234\,5\ldots + 0.987\,659\,876\,5\ldots$ as a fraction.

There are two ways of tackling this – but both methods involve two parts. One approach is to try to add the two decimals to obtain a decimal 'answer'. One must then decide what *fraction* this answer represents. Many candidates did the first step only, and did not translate their 'answer' into a *fraction*.

A4 Three ropes of lengths 8 m, 9 m, 10 m. The arc *AB* is longer than the arcs *BC* and *CA*. Find the length of the arc *AB*.

Since *AB* is the longest arc, it must be part of the two longest ropes.

A5 **Two numbers have difference, sum, and product in the ratio 1 : 4 : 15. What are they?**

It is not hard to find *one* set of numbers that works simply by juggling numbers in your head. But if you manage to find one answer in this way, you cannot be sure that yours is the only answer!

A7 **In a sequence of points, the point (x, y) is followed by $(x + 2y, 2x - y)$. If the first point is (a, b), what is the fifth point?**

Work out the first few terms – but remember that one must always simplify algebraic expressions. When you think you know the answer, try to present your solution completely generally.

A8 ***ABCDEFGH* is a cube of side 3. *X* is one-third of the way along *AB*, *Y* is one-third of the way along *GH*, and *Z* is two-thirds of the way down *DE*. Find the area of triangle *XYZ*.**

The figure is three dimensional, but the triangle *XYZ* is flat. Before you calculate the three lengths *XY*, *YZ*, *ZX*, ask whether you should notice something about these three segments.

A9 **At what time is the angle between the hands of a clock exactly 170°?**

As the time passes from 12 o'clock to 1 o'clock, the angle between the hands increases from $0°$ (at 12 o'clock) to almost $360°$: at 1 o'clock the angle between the hands is exactly _____°. Thus there must be at least one time between 12 and 1 when the angle between the hands is *exactly* 170°. There are in fact *two* times, though they are not that easy to find.

An easier approach is to look for particular times which work. Since 170° is just 10° less than 180°, try to get the hands pointing *almost* in opposite directions: this is easiest if one hand points exactly at an hour mark. But remember, we want *exact* answers. (There are two 'easy' times. Can you find them both?)

A10 **In how many different ways can one pay 20p using standard British coins (1p, 2p, 5p, 10p, 20p)?**

There are many ways of tackling this question, but the key point is to work *systematically* – otherwise, after much hard work you can all too easily end up with the wrong answer.

1993: Section B

There is no such thing as a completely unambiguous problem in mathematics. Every mathematical problem has to be *interpreted*. This may be because you are not entirely familiar with the language: for example, what is meant by the 'vertices' of a cube in question **B1** below. Or perhaps the question is asking you to do something you have never done before (as may have been the case in question **A7** above, or in question **B2** below).

Nevertheless, if you can stay calm and think about such problems carefully, you will often see that *almost everything can be sorted out*, and that what is left unclear need not worry you. Thus, for example, the rest of question **B1** more or less tells you that 'vertices' is another name for 'corners'. Similarly, in question **B2** you may at first wonder whether the year '1900' is in 'this century' or not: if it is, you should count it; if not, you should count the year 2000 instead. In the end it may make no difference. But if it does, and *if the question is genuinely ambiguous*, your solution should include a clear statement of how you have interpreted the question.

B1 **Place 1–8 at vertices of a cube with each face having the same sum. What do you notice about the two numbers at *A* and *B* and the two numbers at *C* and *D*? Explain.**

There are so many ways of labelling the cube that you can't fail to find one labelling that works! (For example, if you number the vertices round the top face 1–4, then the vertices round the bottom face 5–8, it is not hard to do this so that all the vertical faces have the same sum. You should then be able to adjust your labelling to fix the top and bottom faces without messing up the vertical faces!) Hence the interesting part of question **B1** is the second part – to discover what seems to be true and to give a clear, general reason why it *has* to happen.

B2 **31.3.93 is an 'interesting' date since $31 \times 3 = 93$. If all dates are written like this, how many years of the twentieth century contain no interesting dates at all?**

Far too many students just presented lists with *no reasons*. Almost all lists were partly wrong; in the absence of reasons, these inevitably scored very little. You are *not* asked to find *all* interesting dates. You only need to find years which contain *no interesting dates at all*: this is much easier. Once you understand why, you should try exploring *systematically*, keeping your wits about you in the hope you will be able to see what is going on.

First idea: Mmmm! January seems to deal with all years up to _____; February then deals with all . . .

Second idea: What is it about a year that prevents it from having interesting dates? (You should realise that this has something to do with ∗∗i∗e numbers.)

B3 (a) **A 2 by 2 square has semicircles drawn on each edge as shown. The overlaps create four shaded 'petals'. Find the shaded area.**

 (b) **A regular hexagon with sides of length 2 has semicircles drawn on each side (pointing inwards as before). Find the total area of the six 'petals'.**

 (a) The four semicircles cover the whole square, creating exactly four petals. How many times does each petal get covered? You should now be able to calculate the shaded area.

 (b) The method outlined above for part (a) is fine; but it does not generalise to part (b) (since the six semicircles in a regular hexagon *leave a hole uncovered* in the middle of the hexagon). An approach to part (a) which does generalise is to mark the midpoints of the top edge and the right-hand edge and then to focus on the 1 by 1 square in the top right-hand corner of the given 2 by 2 square.

B4 **Does there exist a four-digit perfect square '*aabb*'?**

The word 'square' has two meanings: here we are not dealing with geometrical figures, but with whole numbers.

If you think clearly, problems of this kind are rarely as hard as they look. You are certainly not expected to guess. We want to see *reasoning*. One approach would be to say that any such number must lie between 1100 and 9999, so its square root must lie between _____ and _____. You could then try all numbers in this range. This approach uses some insight, but then resorts to *brute force* in checking lots of possibilities. A little thought about any number of the form '*aabb*' should suggest that any such number has to be a multiple of _____, and so (if it is to be a square) must be a multiple of _____. The answer 'Yes' would only be interesting if it was accompanied by an example, together with a calculation to show that it was indeed a square. However, if your answer happens to be 'No', you must explain clearly why there can be no such square.

B5 (a) Which pairs of numbers a, b satisfy $a + b = a \times b$?
    (b) Can you find three numbers a, b, c such that $a + b + c = a \times b \times c$? Four numbers? Five? . . .

(a) If you are tempted to use trial and error, you might just find some other pairs a, b – though you would never find them all. In fact, if you use trial and error you are most likely to decide that the only obvious pair is $a = 2$, $b = 2$. Whether you find other examples or not, you must at some stage use some algebra to try to find all possible solutions.

(b) The dots at the end suggest we are really being asked to find some general way of producing lists of n numbers whose sum is equal to their product.

B6 *ABCD* is a square with centre O. A' is the midpoint of AO, and B', C', D' are the midpoints of BO, CO, DO respectively. The two parallelograms *AB'CD'* and *A'BC'D* overlap. How big is this overlap as a fraction of the square *ABCD*?

This is a toughie, but a very beautiful toughie. You *must* draw a diagram! You must then look to mark in extra points or lines that might help you solve the problem. The overlap is an octagon, but it is *not* a regular octagon! However, it is made up of eight identical pieces, and this should help.

1992 Section A

A1 Which multiple of 11 is nearest to 1000?

A *multiple* is a number. Thus 22 is a multiple of 11, with *multiplier* 2: 2 is *not* a multiple of 11. Thus the answer to question **A1** is *not* 91.

A3 What is the smallest number which is the sum of two primes in two ways?

Each *odd* number can be written in *at most one way* (Why?). So we only need to test *even* numbers in turn, using a list of small primes $(2, 3, 5, 7, 11, 13, \ldots)$.

A4 On holiday I always wear pants, shorts, T-shirt and sunglasses. I have to put on the T-shirt before the sunglasses, and the pants before the shorts. Each day I dress in a different order. For how long can I keep this up?

I get dressed in four stages. Think about these as Stage 1, Stage 2, Stage 3, Stage 4. 'Pants' and 'shorts' use up two of these stages, and they have to go that way round (Why?), and then the other two stages have to be used for 'T-shirt' and 'sunglasses' (that way round!). How many ways are there to choose two stages? (Answer: _____, namely 12, 13, 14, 23, _____, and _____).

A5 The first term is $\frac{3}{8}$; if x is any term, the next is $\frac{(1-x)}{(1+x)}$. What is the eighth term?

$1 - \frac{3}{8} =$ _____, and $1 + \frac{3}{8} =$ _____; thus the second term = _____.
$1 - \frac{5}{11} =$ _____, and $1 + \frac{5}{11} =$ _____, so the third term = _____!!!
So the fourth term = _____ . . .

A6 Four pipes of diameter 1 m are tied in a 'square' shape by a band. How long is the band?

The four curved bits are all quarter circles, so together they make a whole $*i***e$ of radius $\frac{1}{2}$ m, so of length _____. The four straight bits are tangent to the pipes, so each has length equal to two radii (= one $*ia*e*e*$).

(**Note:** Answers and calculations should always be *exact* – using symbols, fractions or surds where appropriate.)

A7 In question A6 what is the cross-sectional area of the hole between the four pipes?

The cross-section of each pipe is a $*i***e$. The centres of these circles are not marked – so mark them yourself! If you join the centres of each pair of touching pipes you get a $**ua*e$ of side length _____. This has area _____. To get the cross-sectional area of the shaded hole you have to remove the four corners – each of which is a quarter $*i***e$; these four quadrants fit together to make a circle.

A8 My children are all at school and the product of their ages is 60 060. How many children do I have?

If a number is obtained as a product, then the first thing you should want to do is to $*a**o*i*e$ it. How? Always start by factorising it as a product of $**i*e$ $*u**e**$:

$60\,060 =$ __ $\times$ __ $\times$ __ $\times$ __ $\times$ __ $\times$ _____ $\times$ _____. (You should remember something about the factors of 1001 from question **A1**.) Since my children are at school their ages must be between _____ and _____. Sadly this does not tell you how old my children are, but it does determine how many children I have.

(**Note:** Candidates who answered 'Too many' may have been right, but got no marks!)

A9 If I stand with one foot each side of the Equator, how fast am I moving?

In 24 hours I travel 2π ?? km, hence $\dfrac{(2\pi ??)}{24} = \dfrac{(\pi ??)}{12}$ km per hour.

But to stop there is a cop out, because you cannot really tell at a glance how fast this is; whereas the question explicitly asks 'at what approximate speed?'.

A10 29.2.92 is palindromic. How many palindromic dates are there between 1910 and 1999?

You could try to answer 'How many?' by writing out all possibilities and then counting them. But that's book-keeping, not maths! You will almost certainly make mistakes, and won't even notice! For mathematics you need an *idea*.

At first it is not clear *how* to count. The example shows that single digits, like 2, must be written as '2', not '02': so there will be no palindromic dates in 1910 (Why not?). In 1911, each palindromic date looks like ?/?/11. So the number of the day in the month must be _____, and the number of the month must be *a*i***o*i*. Thus the only possible month numbers are _____, _____, _____, _____, _____, _____, _____, _____, or _____, so there are exactly _____ such dates in 1911. The same is true in 1912 (Why?). But 1913 is different (Why? How many palindromic dates are there in 1913?). And 1914 has none at all (Why not?). How many years are there like 1911 and 1912? And how many years like 1913?

1992: Section B

B1 Can the difference between '*ab*' and its reverse '*ba*' ever be a prime number?

It is not enough to try out a few numbers and to 'spot a pattern'. If we start with 74, we get $74 - 47 =$ _____. But the answer is not nearly as important as *how the answer arises* from the original numbers. (Treat the tens and units separately so that $74 - 47 = (7 \times 10 - 4 \times 10) + (4 - 7) =$ _____ $\times 10 -$ _____ $=$ _____ $\times$ _____.)

B2 ABCDEFGH is a regular octagon. How big is $\angle ADG$?

It should not take too long to decide what the answer has to be (it is certainly less than $90°$, and had better not be too unfamiliar!). However, the challenge here is to calculate the value of $\angle ADG$ exactly using only the fact that *ABCDEFGH* is a *regular* octagon. In a regular octagon all the sides have the same length $AB = BC = CD = \ldots$, and all the angles have the same size $\angle ABC = \angle BCD = \angle CDE = \ldots$ The first thing you have to decide is 'How big is each angle in a regular octagon?'.

B3 A sequence begins 1, 1, . . . Each new term is obtained by adding the inverses of the two previous terms and then taking the inverse of the answer. Find the eighth term and explain, with proof, how the sequence continues.

If you calculate the eighth term correctly, simplifying the fractions you get at each stage, you should certainly discover what seems to be happening. However, it is not enough just to *describe* how you think the sequence continues; you have to give a general *proof*.

The third term is obtained by adding the inverses of the first two terms ($\frac{1}{1} + \frac{1}{1}$ = _____), and then taking the inverse of the answer to get _____. Thus the sequence begins $\frac{1}{1}, \frac{1}{1}, \frac{1}{2}, \ldots$ Now suppose $\frac{1}{x}$ and $\frac{1}{y}$ are two successive terms in the sequence (so x and y are the inverses of the actual terms); then use algebra to calculate the next term.

B4 Find the surface area of a cube which just fits in a sphere of radius 1 cm.

Think carefully about how a cube 'fits' inside a sphere: the centre of the cube is at the centre of the sphere, and the eight corners of the cube just touch the surface of the sphere: the top four touch somewhere near the 'Tropic of Cancer', and the bottom four touch somewhere near the 'Tropic of Capricorn'. Draw a reasonable diagram to show this. You are told the radius of the sphere, so you know the distance from the centre of the cube to each of its corners. You have to calculate (exactly!) the length x of one of the edges of the cube.

B5 (a) Which primes can be expressed as the difference of two squares?
(b) Which primes can be so expressed in two or more different ways?

Let the two square numbers be m^2 and n^2. Then their difference $m^2 - n^2$ can always be factorised: $m^2 - n^2 = (\ldots)(\ldots)$. This is one of the two most useful facts of elementary algebra! If $m^2 - n^2$ is to be a prime number, one of the two factors on the right-hand side (RHS) must be equal to 1.

B6 **Find the area of the shaded region.**

You have to calculate exactly. To find the required area, you would first like to calculate some lengths. Fortunately there are lots of right-angled triangles, so you should expect to use Pythagoras' theorem.

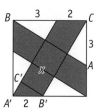

Unfortunately, you only seem to know *one side* in each right-angled triangle! Clearly another idea is needed – namely, that all the right-angled triangles in the diagram are ∗i∗i∗a∗ to one another.

1991: Section A

A1 **What is the largest prime factor of 1991?**

The question asks for the *largest*, not the smallest, prime factor of 1991. The middle two digits 99 positively beg you to try _____ as a possible prime factor. In fact 1991 = 11 × _____.

A2 **If Ann earns £$\frac{5}{6}$ per $\frac{4}{5}$ hour and Ben earns £$\frac{7}{8}$ per $\frac{6}{7}$ hour, how long must Ann and Ben work (as a team) to earn £66?**

Ann and Ben work as a *team*, so 'how long' must refer to how long *the team* works – not the sum of their individual work times. If Ann were paid £x for y hours, how much would she be paid per hour? Obviously £$\frac{x}{y}$. Use this to work out what the team gets paid per hour. Then see how many hours they must work to earn £66.

A3 **In the square $ABCD$, M bisects BC and N bisects AD. The circle centre N through M cuts CD at P. Find $\angle PNM$.**

The crucial observation here is that if the circle through M, with centre N, cuts CD at P and AB at Q, then triangle NPQ is e∗ui∗a∗e∗a∗.

A4 **Find a number less than 100 which increases by 20% when its digits are reversed.**

If the number is to 'increase by 20%' (that is, one-fifth), it had better be exactly divisible by _____, so must have units digit equal to _____. The tens digit must be smaller than the units digit (Why?). That does not leave many possibilities.

A5 Each semicircle has radius 1 cm. Find the total area enclosed.

Each semicircular bump can be cut off and used to fill the opposite dent. Thus the problem is really about finding the area of a regular *e*a*o* with sides of length _____ cm.

A6 Razia broke her necklace. She found one-third of the beads on the floor, one-quarter in her pocket, one-fifth down the side of the sofa, while one-sixth remained on the string; six beads were never found. How many beads were there to start with?

Let the number of beads originally on the necklace be b. Then use the information to set up an equation.

A7 The points A, B, C, D, E and F are at the 12, 2, 3, 6, 8 and 9 o'clock hour marks on a clockface. Find the ratio of the area of $ABDE$ to the area of $ACDF$.

Far too many candidates confused *lengths* and *angles*, giving the required ratio as 8 : 9. (The *angle AOB* is indeed *two*-twelfths of 360°, and the *angle BOD* is *four*-twelfths of 360°; but one cannot multiply these to get the area of $ABDE$ as if AB were 'two units' *long* and BD were 'four units' *long*.)
The required ratio does not depend on the size of the clockface (why not?), so we can let the radius equal 2. The length AC should be easy to find. To find AB you need to recognise equilateral triangles again: this should be part of the stock-in-trade of anyone interested in mathematics. One way of finding the length BD is to recognise the triangle BOP as half of the (equilateral!) triangle BOG.

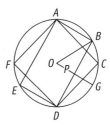

A8 The first two terms of a sequence are a and b. Each new term is obtained by dividing the previous term by the one before that. What is the eighth term in the sequence?

It is no good simply generating the sequence according to the given rules:

$$a, \quad b, \quad b \div a, \quad (b \div a) \div b, \quad ((b \div a) \div b) \div (b \div a),$$
$$(((b \div a) \div b) \div (b \div a)) \div ((b \div a) \div b), \ldots$$

53

The goal of mathematics is *not* just to be formally correct, but to discover *meaning*. Algebra is meaningful only if one always insists on *simplifying*. The whole point of the question is to notice first that the fourth term can be considerably *simplified*. This art of simplification is the mathematician's most precious tool. Only by simplifying intelligently is it possible to discover the amazing things that lie concealed in a morass of symbols. In this case, when you simplify, you will discover something totally unexpected.

A9 **A net for a pyramid has a square base of side length 10 cm with an equilateral triangle on each side of the square. What will be the height of the pyramid after it has been made?**

In the pyramid you should see right-angled triangles all over the place. The square base has diagonals of length $\sqrt{\underline{\hspace{1.5cm}}}$. So the distance from a corner to the centre of the base is $\sqrt{\underline{\hspace{1.5cm}}}$. Now find another right-angled triangle that will help you to calculate the height of the finished pyramid.

A10 **In how many ways can 105 equal the sum of consecutive positive integers?**

There are lots! If *two* consecutive numbers are to add to 105, their average must be _____, so we get $105 = \underline{\hspace{1cm}} + \underline{\hspace{1cm}}$. If *three* consecutive numbers are to add to 105, their average must be _____, so we get $105 = \underline{\hspace{1cm}} + \underline{\hspace{1cm}} + \underline{\hspace{1cm}}$. And so on.

1991: Section B

B1 **Find the shortest and longest gaps between successive palindromic years.**

When a mathematical problem refers to the 'shortest and longest *possible* gaps' it is asking you to use your imagination. You must not force things to fit a simple pattern. Any simple pattern for palindromic years breaks down when the number of digits in the year goes up by one, so that we get a very small 'gap' from, say, 999 to _____, or from 9999 to _____.

Many candidates realised that they should *not* restrict attention to years with four digits, or even ten digits. However, too many made the mistake of simply saying: 'Since the possible number of years is infinite, the biggest gap will be infinite.' This assertion is logically quite wrong, and in two ways. There can never be an *infinite* gap between successive palindromic years. And if you want to show that the gap can be *arbitrarily big*, you have to produce, **for each n**, two successive palindromic years with a gap bigger than (say) 10^n.

B2 **How many years since AD 1 (up to 1991) used just two different digits?**

Mathematics is not just about answers. So even though this problem appears to ask for an answer, what matters is *how you work it out*. You must therefore explain your method as clearly as you can. This has the extra advantage that you might realise which bit of the problem is the tricky bit.

Counting years with two digits shouldn't be too hard, though surprisingly many candidates (a) think there are 89 years from 10 to 99, and (b) include 100 along with the two-digit years, which makes mathematical counting difficult.

Counting years with three digits is a wee bit harder! And counting four-digit years is almost impossible *unless you have a systematic mathematical way of doing it*. Too few candidates seemed to realise this, and so ploughed on with simple-minded methods. These methods were almost bound to produce wrong answers; and grinding out answers in this way is both unsatisfying and mathematically unsatisfactory – since even if you know that the answer is wrong (and those who landed up with answers like 6573 years should really have twigged!), there is no way of finding out where you have gone wrong. So you have to find a way of counting the four-digit years systematically and reliably.

B3 **(a)** **Find the next perfect square after 9 that is equal to the sum of two different cubes.**
  (b) **Can a perfect square ever be written as the sum of three squares?**

  (a) It is important to be able to search systematically and efficiently for numbers, or combinations of numbers, which have certain properties. $4^2 = 2^3 + 2^3$ does not answer the question (Why not?). Neither does $9^2 = 3^3 + 4^3$ (though hundreds of candidates seemed to think it did).
  When you first meet the problem, one perfectly sensible approach is to write down a list of squares 1, 4, 9, 16, 25, 36, 49, 64, . . . and a list of cubes 1, 8, 27, 64, 125, . . . and search systematically (and accurately!). But don't give up too soon!
  And when you do find 'the next perfect square which can be written as a sum of two cubes', don't just write it down, but look carefully at what you have found to see if you could have found it much more quickly!

  (b) Far too many candidates failed to read the question carefully, and simply tried to write a square as the sum of three *cubes*. (Lots of these wrote something like $16 = 8 + 8 + 0$ and left it at that! Even if the question had asked you to write a square as the sum of three cubes, you should want to go on to see whether you can find three non-zero cubes whose sum is a square.)

55

B4 **For which values of N can an N-gon have successive sides always equal in length and at right angles?**

As always, the question needs to be read carefully and interpreted sensibly. A polygon in which all *internal* angles are right angles has to be a *rectangle*! Thus the question *cannot* be referring to internal angles only. If you now read the question carefully, you will see that it only says successive sides are 'at right angles'. Two further points were overlooked by many candidates. The question says quite clearly that the N sides all have 'the same $*e****$').

(If you allow sides of *different* lengths, then it is not hard to construct a hexagon – such as the one on the right.)

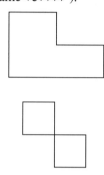

At some point you may have to decide whether two squares with only a vertex in common can really be counted as a 'polygon with eight sides'. In fact, it is an important part of the *definition* of a polygon that the sides do not cross, and that only two sides meet at each vertex.

After a while, you should be convinced that there are lots of values of N for which it is possible to construct such a polygon, but that all possible values of N seem to be $e*e*$. Can you *prove* that N cannot be $o**$?

B5 **Two walls, one of height a metres and the other of height b metres, are d metres apart. A ladder of length l metres has its feet hinged at a point between the two walls and can just reach the top of each. The two positions of the ladder are at right angles. How many different solutions are there for a, b, d, l if all four have to be positive integers less than 20?**

In such a question you have to start by drawing a careful sketch diagram. (Go on, draw a diagram!) Let A be the point at the bottom of the wall of height a, and let A' be the top. Let B be the point at the bottom of the wall of height b, and let B' be the top. Let H be the point where the ladder is hinged. Very few candidates noticed the basic fact about the angles AHA' and BHB'. What is it? What does this tell you about the two triangles $A'AH$ and HBB'?

B6 Eebs have honeycombs with square cells, all packed tightly together. An eeb grub starts in one cell. Each day it moves to a neighbouring cell, possibly revisiting a cell it occupied on a previous occasion.

(a) Suppose it starts in a cell in the middle of the honeycomb. How many different cells would you have to look in to be sure of finding it on the nth day?

(b) What if the grub starts in a corner cell as shown here? How many different cells would you have to look in to be sure of finding it on the nth day?

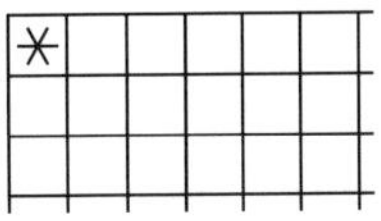

If you read the question carefully, you will realise that the eeb cannot stay in the same cell ('each day it *moves* to a neighbouring cell').

The word 'neighbouring' should make you think. Do 'neighbouring' cells have to have a whole edge in common? Or do they merely have to have a corner in common? A moment's thought might suggest that the eeb would find it much easier, and much more natural, to move to a genuine 'neighbouring' cell, that is one which had a *wall* in common with it. But whenever there is a doubt in your mind, it is worth asking which is the *more interesting* question.

In this case, if you interpret 'neighbouring' in one way, the number of cells you would have to look in for both part (a) and part (b) is (boringly) easy, but if you interpret it the other way, the problem becomes much more interesting!

1990: Section A

A1 1990 is ten times a prime number. What is the next number like this?

Not 10×201 (Why not?). Nor 10×203 (Why not?).

A2 How many 6 cm by 8 cm tickets can one cut out of a 30 cm by 21 cm card?

The 30 cm by 21 cm card has area _____ cm², and each ticket has area _____ cm². Now it is true (and relevant) that $630 \div 48 = $ '13 and a bit'. But this does not mean that the answer to the question is 13: all it tells you is that you *cannot possibly get 14* tickets out of the given piece of card.

A3 How many prime numbers less than 10 000 have digits adding to 2?

There aren't many possibilities! There's 2 itself. And 11. And ...?

A4 The corners of a regular hexagon (in order) are *P, Q, R, S, T, U. PT* and *SU* cross at the point *V*. How big is the angle *TVS*?

The hexagon is a *mathematical* hexagon – not a wooden one. And the question is a *mathematical* question, not one asked by a carpenter. So protractors are useless! You want to know the *exact* size of the perfect *mathematical* angle, so you must use perfect mathematical calculations.

A5 The digit 3 is written at the right of a certain two-digit number to make a three-digit number. The new number is 777 more than the original two-digit number. What was the original number?

'ab3' = 'ab' + '777'. This tells you what *b* has to be.

A6 An equilateral triangle and a regular hexagon have equal perimeters. Find the ratio of their areas.

Simple properties of equilateral triangles and regular hexagons are part of the stock-in-trade of young mathematicians. At least, they *should* be!

A7 How far forward should the runner in the outside lane start in a one-lap race round a six-lane track (each lane 1 metre wide)?

To obtain clear and precise answers one has to interpret the question and make sensible assumptions. How far forward of *what*? What shape is the track? Once you sort these out, you should begin to see how to calculate how much longer the outside lane is than the inside lane.

A8 The sun is 60° above the horizon. A vertical tree, 60 ft high, casts its shadow straight down a 30° slope. How long is the shadow?

The sun, the tree, and the shadow beg you to draw a diagram: far too many candidates didn't! You should then realise that all that stuff about 30° and 60° means this is really a question about e∗ui∗a∗e∗a∗ triangles.

A9 A new operation ⋆ for combining two numbers *a* and *b* is defined by
$$a \star b = \frac{(a+b)}{2}.$$
If $x \star (x \star 14) = x$, what is *x*?

Are you sure you read the question? ⋆ does *not* mean 'multiply'. The question tells you that $a \star b = \frac{(a+b)}{2}$; that is, $a \star b$ is the a∗e∗a∗e (or ∗ea∗) of the two numbers *a* and *b*.

58

A10 **The sun rises at 04:43 in London. When does it rise in Cardiff (3° W)?**

Draw a diagram! (What sort of diagram?) And mark important points, like L (= London), C (= Cardiff), and S (= the sun). At L (= London) the sun is just rising (in the east!). How should you represent this? You want to know when it will rise at C (= Cardiff).

1990: Section B

B1 **In how many ways can the word 'MATHS' be traced out in this diagram if you are only allowed to move one step at a time horizontally or vertically, up or down, backwards or forwards?**

```
              S
            S H S
          S H T H S
        S H T A T H S
      S H T A M A T H S
        S H T A T H S
          S H T H S
            S H S
              S
```

If you just try to count all the possibilities by tracing them with your pen you will mess up the diagram and you are *bound to make a mistake*. You will then score zero and have absolutely nothing to show for your efforts. Thus you need a mathematical *idea* to break the problem into manageable bits.

B2 **'y pounds and x pence' minus one pound is twice 'x pounds and y pence'. Find x, y.**

The first task is to use the information given to set up an equation. y pounds and x pence is equal to _____ pence. After spending £1, that leaves _____ pence. And we are told that this is twice as much as the man originally asked for. Write this information as an equation linking x and y.

B3 **Which numbers cannot be made up exactly using a combination of 5s, 9s, and 12s?**

A 'combination of coins' suggests clearly that we are only allowed to *add* 5s, 9s and 12s. Trial and error can be a good way of getting started, but *be systematic*: 1, 2, 3 and 4 are clearly impossible; 5 is OK; 6–8 are impossible; 9 is OK; 10 is OK; 11 is impossible; 12 is OK; . . .

If you keep your wits about you, systematic trial and error may lead you to stumble upon a complete solution. But for this to happen

- you have to be *looking* for a complete solution, and
- you must know the difference between experimental evidence and proof.

59

It is no good at all drawing up a table which seems to show that every number from some point on can be obtained if you then just *assume* this is the answer. How can you be sure that *all* numbers in the millions or beyond can be made?

(**Note:** If you allow 'giving change' – that is, subtraction as well as addition – then everything is possible, so the question loses a lot of its interest.)

B4 **A cylindrical barrel of diameter 1 metre lies on its side right up against a wall. How big a ball will fit in the gap between the barrel and the wall?**

Draw a clear diagram and then look at it carefully. If P is the point where the wall and floor meet, if O is the centre of the barrel, and A is the point where the segment OP meets the barrel, then the diameter of the ball is definitely *not* $OP - OA = AP$. (Why not?)

B5 (a) **$3^2 = 9$ is very nearly the average of two other squares. Find them.**
   (b) **Find three squares where one is exactly the average of the other two. Show that there are infinitely many such triples.**

(a) The other squares must have sum roughly equal to _____. So what are they?
   We all need to practise our ability to juggle numbers and ideas in our heads (just as a violinist needs to practise scales and arpeggios).

(b) It is certainly worth trying to do the first part *in your head* (it's not hard). But if you have difficulty, by all means jot down a list of squares;

   $1^2 =$ _____, $2^2 =$ _____, $3^2 =$ _____, $4^2 =$ _____, . . .
   (up to, say, $15^2 =$ _____).

   Then check *systematically*. However, it is the last part that is the most interesting part of question **B5**, so don't just calculate blindly.

B6 (a) **How many winning lines in 4 by 4 noughts and crosses? *n* by *n*?**

Questions which challenge you to work out 'How many . . .?' can be an excellent way of experiencing something of the flavour of real mathematics. On the surface it looks as though all you have to do is to *count*. So if you aren't careful, before your brain gets a chance to warm up, out come the fingers – or what is roughly the same, a picture of a noughts-and-crosses board with pen lines drawn all over it. I repeat:

> *trying to count like that is (lousy) book-keeping, not mathematics.*

Mathematics is the science of how to calculate *reliably*! That means you have to look for an idea which will help you *know* that you have not missed anything, and that will *guarantee insight* – so that, for example, a 100 by 100 game of noughts and crosses is no more difficult than a 3 by 3 game. To deal with an *n* by *n* game of noughts and crosses we are going to need a little a**e**a. Many students have quite the wrong idea about algebra. It is *completely useless* to count the number of winning lines

> first on a 3 by 3 board,
>
> then on a 4 by 4 board,
>
> then on a 5 by 5 board,

and then to try to find a formula which 'fits' your answers. *That is not mathematics.* Not only will it give the wrong answer in all but the simplest cases, but you will have no way of knowing whether the 'answer' you get is right or wrong! In mathematics we have to try to uncover *the truth*. Mathematics is not a game in which human beings get marks for trying to guess correctly. We must look for *insight*, not mere guesses.

So if algebra is not about guessing the *n*th term (by working out the first, second, and third terms, . . ., and then trying to see a 'pattern') what on earth is it about? If guessing is unacceptable as a final method, what can provide the necessary insight? The answer is very simple. Algebra is a way of capturing *complete generality of method by using symbols to represent the general case.* In this problem, the general case is an *n* by *n* game of noughts and crosses. We *gain insight* into the *general* case by studying particular cases *in the right way*.

So you must

> try to count the winning lines on a 3 by 3 and a 4 by 4 board
>
> *in a way which will help you count winning lines on an n by n board.*

This may not be easy. But it is not too difficult either.

1989

1 Find the smallest multiple of 9 with no odd digits.

You could just write out all multiples of 9 until you find one with no odd digits. This approach is not satisfactory, and tends to lead to rather basic errors: for example, stopping as soon as you get to 18 (because of the 8), or to 99 (because your experience of number is limited to the 10 by 10 number square, so that 99 is the biggest familiar multiple of 9), or to 108 (because of the two even digits). One reason such a bare hands approach is *unmathematical* is that it is all too easy to *make a mistake* when adding 9 over and over again *and not to notice*!

A more mathematical approach is to notice that
(i)   9 is odd, so if all digits are to be even, we only need worry about e*e* multiples of 9 – that is, *multiples of 18*;
(ii) every multiple of 9 up to 100 has either an odd tens digit, or an odd units digit;
(iii) every multiple of 9 from 100 to 199 has an odd hundreds digit.

Thus we need only worry about multiples of 18 above _____.

2 The two small semicircles inside the big circle divide the big circle into two congruent pieces. Explain how to cut the shaded and unshaded regions exactly in half with a single straight cut.

Many candidates merely drew a line on a rough diagram, with no precise indication of where this line should go. You have to say *exactly* where the line should go, and *why your answer is correct*.

3 How could you multiply 7 628 954 301 by 125 in your head?

Most candidates did not read the question, and proceeded to describe (at great length) how they would do the calculation on paper!

Some improved on this slightly (for example: add two 0s on the end – to get 100 times; then divide this by 4 – to get 25 times; then add the two answers). But doing either of these in your head would require you to remember two or more 12-digit numbers!

4 Joining each vertex in the big regular hexagon to the next vertex but one produces a smaller hexagon inside. Prove that the smaller hexagon is regular. Find its edge length in terms of the edge length of the big hexagon.

Far too many candidates thought this question could be answered using a ruler. It can't! In mathematics you cannot prove anything by *measuring*. Mathematics is about *imaginary* triangles, hexagons, etc. We use drawings, sketches, and figures only to help us *think* about imaginary, perfect figures. Measuring can be useful

(i) as an introduction to theoretical geometry, where one has to learn that the objects of theoretical geometry are *ideal* lines and lengths and angles, not the lines you draw and measure with a ruler, and

(ii) in practical applications of geometry – though even there you must first understand the theoretical geometry which lies behind your construction.

Students may realise all this, yet still not understand quite what is meant by the word *prove*. In this instance a *proof* should combine *in a very precise way*

(i) what you are *told* about the big hexagon – namely that it is *regular*, and

(ii) general geometrical results (such as that the base angles of an isosceles triangle are always equal).

Starting out from *what you know is true*, you must then proceed *one step at a time* until you manage to *deduce the result you want to prove*.

5 Find two perfect squares that differ by 105. How many different solutions are there?

Remember that these problems should be done *without a calculator*. If you are interested in mathematics, you have to learn to juggle numbers in your head. Finding one pair of squares that differ by exactly 105 should not be too hard (there are two such squares less than $12^2 = 144$).

6 A right-angled triangle has legs of length a and b. A circle of radius r touches the two legs and has its centre on the hypotenuse. Show that

$$\frac{1}{a} + \frac{1}{b} = \frac{1}{r}.$$

This question may contain a couple of words you don't immediately recognise, but you should be able to work out what they mean. Some words you should certainly *know*: for example, you should know what 'right-angled triangle' means, and what 'hypotenuse' means.

But what about 'legs'? Even if you do not know what they are, the question says they have 'length a and b', so they must be *sides of the triangle*; and (since we have already met the hypotenuse) they must be the two *shorter* sides of the triangle. And what about that word 'touches'? What must it mean for a *circle* to 'touch' a *line*? Clearly the circle must meet the line in some way. But a circle which meets a line either *cuts it* in two places, or is *tangent* to the line. Which of these could be described by the word 'touch'? There is really only one possible answer. Many candidates drew the *wrong* diagram – with the circle going through the vertices of the triangle, rather than 'touching the sides'. Of those who drew the correct diagram, very few drew in the *two really important lines* (both of length r), which would have shown that this question is really about *similar right-angled triangles*. Draw in these two important lines and finish off the question.

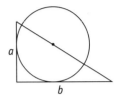

7 **Find all pairs (x, y) whose sum, product, and quotient are all equal.**

You clearly have to solve the equations $x + y = x.y = \frac{x}{y}$. It is tempting to try to stick to *whole* numbers. But no one said that the solutions have to be whole numbers, or even positive numbers.

You may be tempted to suggest $x = 0$, $y = 0$ as one solution. But what does $\frac{0}{0}$ mean? In mathematics *dividing by 0 is forbidden* – it makes no sense! (Can you see why?) Thus y cannot be 0. Could $x = 0$?

8 **An equilateral triangle with sides of length 3 is cut into nine equilateral triangles of side length 1. Place the numbers 1 to 9 in the nine small triangles so that the sum of the numbers inside any equilateral triangle with side length 2 is the same. What are the smallest and largest possible values of this sum?**

Trial and error may help you to get a feeling for the problem. But it is no good just looking for the 'smallest' and 'largest' totals you happen to find. Instead you must look for an *idea* that will convince everyone else that *they* could never improve on your totals.

9 If $a^2 + b^2 + c^2 = ab + bc + ca$, must a, b, c all be equal?

This question proved to be rather hard! It is not really a question about triangles at all. The three numbers a, b, c are lengths, and so must be *positive real numbers*. To prove that triangle ABC must be 'equilateral', it is enough to prove that $a = b = c$. This is all that matters.

10 Pythagoras' theorem for the right-angled triangle ABC is often illustrated by a diagram like the one shown here (without the dotted lines). Putting in the three dotted lines shows that the whole figure can be enclosed in a hexagon. Find the area of this hexagon in terms of the edge lengths a, b, c of the original triangle

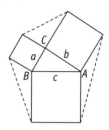

The diagram shows the hexagon split into $*e*e*$ separate bits; this positively invites you to work out the area of each bit separately – and then add them all up. Five of the bits are easy. So the real problem is to calculate the areas of each of the other two bits.

11 (a) Find a square (other than 5^2, 10^2, 15^2, . . .) which is the sum of two squares.

Intelligent searching is an important part of mathematics. A list of squares is likely to be useful, so jot them down:

$$1^2 = \underline{\hspace{1cm}}, \quad 2^2 = \underline{\hspace{1cm}}, \quad 3^2 = \underline{\hspace{1cm}}, \quad 4^2 = \underline{\hspace{1cm}},$$

$$5^2 = \underline{\hspace{1cm}}, \quad 6^2 = \underline{\hspace{1cm}}, \quad 7^2 \underline{\hspace{1cm}}, . . .$$

The squares up to 225 should be engraved on your heart, so you should not have to do much 'calculating' to produce this list.

12 Two straight cuts, one through each of two vertices of a triangle, divide the triangle into three smaller triangles and one quadrilateral.
(a) Is it possible for the areas of all four parts to be equal?
(b) More generally, if three of the parts have area p while the fourth has area q, what are the possible values of $\frac{p}{q}$?

(a) Your first move must be to interpret the question carefully by drawing a diagram. Suppose all four regions could have the same area. Let one of the cuts be the line L. How many regions are there on each side of L? What does this tell you about the areas on each side of L? And what does this tell you about L?

13 Mr and Mrs *A* invite some other married couples to dinner. As they all meet, some pairs shake hands. Married couples do not shake hands with one another. Over coffee, while Mr *A* is washing up, the rest discover that they all shook hands a different number of times.

(a) Suppose there were four couples altogether (including Mr and Mrs *A*). Can you say how many hands Mr *A* must have shaken?

(a) This is not nearly as hard as you might think. However, you do have to read the question carefully.

Outline solutions

These outline solutions are here for you to use. However, they are meant to be used in two rather different ways.

Their first, and most obvious, purpose is to help you when you get well-and-truly stuck! When you try a problem, the wording may at first seem unclear; or the problem may look unfamiliar, or impossibly difficult. But if you keep *trying* to make sense of it, you will usually discover that it is nowhere near as hard as it once seemed. So never give up too easily, and don't be tempted to look up the solution too soon. As a rough guide I suggest that you should never look at the solution to a problem unless you have already made a serious attempt to solve it – spending at least 15 minutes (say) on any Section A problem, and at least 30 minutes on any Section B problem.

The outline solutions also have another function. Even when you think you have managed to solve a problem completely, it is worth taking time to go through the outline solution presented here. You will learn a lot from this – and may even realise that your own 'complete' solution was unsatisfactory in some way.

Most of the outline solutions presented here have 'gaps' for you to fill in. The gaps are there just to keep you on your toes; they are not meant to block your progress. If you read and understand what is written, it should not be difficult to provide the missing steps. This will give you a chance to play an active part in generating both a complete solution and the final answer for yourself.

1995: Section A

A1 **Evaluate 123 123 ÷ 1001.**

Do this twice. First, you should be able to do long division quickly and accurately. Second, fill in the gap in the following calculation:

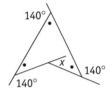

$$1001 \overline{)123123}$$

123 123 = 123 000 + 123 = 123 × 1000 + 123 = 123 × _____.

A2 **What is the size of the angle *x*?**

Two steps are needed. First, the three supplementary angles marked with a dot are all equal to 180° – _____ = _____. Thus we have an arrow-shaped quadrilateral with three angles equal to _____.

Second, you should know that the four angles in any quadrilateral always have sum _____, and the only unknown angle is 180° + *x*. Hence (180° + *x*) + 40° + 40° + 40° = _____, so *x* = _____.

A3 **What is $\dfrac{1}{1 \times 2} + \dfrac{1}{2 \times 3} + \dfrac{1}{3 \times 4} + \dfrac{1}{4 \times 5}$ equal to?**

The denominators 2, 6, 12, 20 have least common multiple _____, so we may rewrite all four fractions with the same denominator 60; $\dfrac{1}{2} = \dfrac{30}{60}$, and so on.

Now add the four fractions to get $\dfrac{?+?+?+?}{60} = $ _____. (Always remember to ∗i∗∗∗i∗y.)

A different, and more interesting, solution arises from putting *n* = 1, 2, 3, 4 in the identity

$$\frac{1}{n(n+1)} = \frac{1}{n} - \frac{1}{n+1}$$

Thus the given sum is really

$$\left(\tfrac{1}{1} - \tfrac{1}{2}\right) + \left(\tfrac{1}{2} - \tfrac{1}{3}\right) + \left(\tfrac{1}{3} - \tfrac{1}{4}\right) + \left(\tfrac{1}{4} - \tfrac{1}{5}\right)$$

All the middle terms cancel in pairs, leaving $1 - \tfrac{1}{5} = $ _____.

A4 **What is the largest amount one can have in standard British coins (1p, 2p, 5p, 10p, 20p, 50p, £1 = 100p), yet still not be able to make exactly £1?**

Observe first that with one 50p and four 20ps we may have £1.30 without being able to make £1. If we have no 50p coins, the most we can have (without having £1) is much less than £1.30 (it is in fact _____); thus we must have at least one 50p coin. Clearly we can have at most _____ 20p coins. If we have no 20p coins, we can have at most four 10p coins and the most we can have altogether (without making £1) is _____; if we have one 20p coin, we can have at most two 10p coins and the most we can have altogether is _____; if we have two 20p coins, we cannot have any 10p coins, so the most we can have altogether is _____; if we have three 20p coins, the most we can have altogether is _____. Hence we must have four 20p coins. Thus the most we can have altogether is if we have _____ 10p coins, _____ 5p coins, _____ 2p coins, and _____ 1p coins.

A5 **Three 'quarter circles' and one 'three-quarter circle' (all of radius 10 cm) make this jug shape. What is its area?**

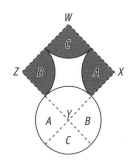

Mark the centres of the four circles and join them as shown. Then shift the three lower quadrants marked A, B, C to complete the square $WXYZ$ with sides of length $XY =$ _____. Hence the original shape has area = _____.

A6 **'Cancelling the two 9s' in $\frac{19}{95}$ is wrong but gives the correct answer $\frac{1}{5}$. Can you find a similar 'false equation' with the correct value $\frac{2}{5}$ on the right-hand side?**

We want $\frac{'2x'}{'x5'} = \frac{2}{5}$; that is '$2x$' × 5 = '$x5$' × 2. The left-hand side lies between 100 and 145; hence the tens digit 'x' on the right-hand side must be either _____ or _____. Only one of these two possibilities works.

(Alternatively, rewrite the equation '$2x$' × 5 = '$x5$' × 2 as $(20 + x)5 = (10x + 5)2$ and solve to get $x =$ _____.)

A7 What is the total area of the shaded region?

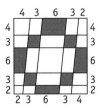

The shaded region consists of six parallelograms and two trapezia. You know the base and height of each parallelogram, so you can calculate all six of these areas exactly to get a subtotal of _____.

The two trapezia may seem more awkward, until you notice that they fit together to make a single rectangle with base _____ and height _____, and hence area = _____. Hence the total area of the shaded region = _____.

A8 How many numbers from 1 to 50 are divisible by neither 5 nor 7, and have neither 5 nor 7 as a digit?

Numbers between 1 and 50 which have 5 as a digit are automatically divisible by 5: there are exactly _____ multiples of 5 which are ≤50. (Remember to count 5 itself!) There are exactly _____ multiples of 7 which are ≤50, and just _____ of these is a multiple of 5 as well, so has already been counted.

It remains to count numbers ≤50 which have 7 as a digit and which have not already been counted. There are exactly _____ numbers ≤50 with 7 as a digit, and exactly _____ of these has already been counted (since it is a multiple of _____).

Adding gives a total of $10 + (7 - 1) + (5 - 1) =$ _____ numbers ≤50 that must be replaced by 'Fizz' or 'Buzz'; so $50 - 20 =$ _____ do not get replaced by 'Fizz' or 'Buzz'.

A9 Given a cube with its eight corners cut off, how many diagonals joining the 24 new 'corners' lie completely inside the cube?

Each new corner C lies on one old edge, so lies in two old square faces, F, F'. C is joined to exactly three other new corners J, P, Q by edges. The diagonals from C to each of the other five new corners K, L, M, N, O in the face F lie on the surface of the cube, as do the diagonals to the other five new corners in the face F'. This leaves diagonals CX from C to exactly $24 - 1 - 3 - (2 \times 5)$ = _____ other new corners X which lie completely inside the cube. The same is true for each of the 24 new corners. Adding we get 24×10, but this counts each diagonal twice, so the required total is _____.

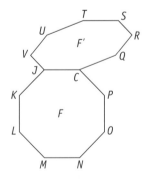

A10 Candles A and B are lit together. Candle A lasts eleven hours, candle B lasts seven hours. After three hours the two candles have equal lengths remaining. Find the ratio of their original lengths.

Suppose the initial length of candle A is a, and that of candle B is b. Candle A lasts 11 hours, so after 3 hours A has length _____. Candle B lasts 7 hours, so after 3 hours B has length _____. Hence $\frac{8}{11}a = \frac{4}{7}b$. Thus

$$b : a = \underline{\quad} : \underline{\quad}.$$

1995: Section B

B1 Take any two-digit number and subtract the sum of the digits. Then divide the answer by 9. What do you find? Explain!

Take any two-digit number 'ab'. Subtract the sum of the digits by first subtracting b (to get '$a0$' $= 10a$), then a (to get $10a - a = 9a$). Finally divide by 9 to get a: the tens digit of the original number. Alternatively 'ab' $= 10a + b$, so 'ab' $- (a+b) = (10a+b) - (a+b) = 9a$, and dividing by 9 gives $\frac{9a}{9} = \underline{\quad}$.

B2 How many times are there, like 21:15, on a digital clock which look the same in a vertical mirror?

Method 1: When you reflect in a mirror, the hours digits become the minutes digits (backwards). Thus there is at most one such time each hour. We can now try each possible pair of hours digits in turn (00:??, 01:??, 02:??, etc.), reflect the hours digits to get the minutes digits, and see which ones work and which do not work.

Method 2: The only digits that reflect to give themselves are _____, _____ and _____. The only digits that reflect to give another digit are _____ and _____. Each digit has to occur with its reflection (one as an hours digit, the other as a minutes digit); the digit 8 can only occur in the second and fourth places, so cannot occur at all. Thus we need only check times involving _____, _____, _____ and _____. There are exactly eleven such times.

(For a digital clock that shows 'ten past one' as 1:10 rather than 01:10, four of the eleven times – namely 00:00, 01:10, 02:50, 05:20 – do not occur.)

B3 **Which of the shaded rectangles has the larger area?**

Given any rectangle $ABCD$, if we draw the diagonal AC we create two triangles ABC and CDA which are identical (the correct word is *congruent*). This is because

$$\angle BAC = \angle DCA \quad \text{(alternate angles, since } AB \text{ is parallel to } DC)$$

$$\angle BCA = \angle DAC \quad \text{(alternate angles, since } BC \text{ is parallel to } AD)$$

$$\text{and} \quad AC = CA \quad \text{(common side)}$$

Thus the 'ASA congruence criterion' shows that $\triangle ABC$ and $\triangle CDA$ are congruent.

In particular, a diagonal always cuts a rectangle into two parts of equal area. We now apply this fact three times.

(i)   In the top left white rectangle, the two parts have equal areas, say x.
(ii) In the bottom right white rectangle, the two parts have equal areas, say y.
(iii) In the large rectangle, the two parts have equal areas, say z.

Hence each of the shaded rectangles has area $z - (x + y)$, so their areas are equal.

This is an excellent example of real mathematics: the solution is completely general, and the unexpected answer ('both shaded rectangles have the same area') is explained in terms of something very simple ('any diagonal cuts a rectangle exactly in half').

B4 **Given any starting number (other than 1), get a new number by dividing the number 1 bigger than your starting number by the number 1 less than your starting number. Then do the same with this new number. What happens? Explain!**

Let the starting number be x. Then the next term is $y = \dfrac{(x+1)}{(x-1)}$. Now take y and work out $\dfrac{(y+1)}{(y-1)}$ the hard way:

$$y = \frac{x+1}{x-1} = \frac{(x-1)+2}{x-1} = 1 + \frac{2}{x-1}$$

$$\therefore y + 1 = 2 + \frac{2}{x-1} \quad \text{and} \quad y - 1 = \frac{2}{x-1}$$

$$\therefore \frac{y+1}{y-1} = \frac{2 + \frac{2}{x-1}}{\frac{2}{x-1}} = \frac{2}{\frac{2}{x-1}} + 1 = (x-1) + 1 = \underline{\qquad}.$$

$$\left[\text{Alternatively, } \frac{y+1}{y-1} = \frac{\frac{(x+1)}{(x-1)} + 1}{\frac{(x+1)}{(x-1)} - 1} = \frac{(x+1)+(x-1)}{(x+1)-(x-1)} = \frac{2x}{2} = x. \right]$$

B5 **Nine squares are arranged to form a rectangle as shown. The smallest square has sides of length 1. How big is the next smallest square?**

Let A have sides of length a, B have sides of length b, etc.

From the diagram we see that $a < b$, $a < c < d < i$, $a < f < g < h$; also $e < f < g < b < h$, and $e < c < d < i$. Hence A and E are the two smallest squares.

Now $b = a + g$, $c = a + b = 2a + g$, $f = g - a$, and $c + a = f + e$,

so $e = c + a - f = c + a - (g - a) = (2a + g) + a - g + a = 4a$.

Since $a = 1$, we have $e = \underline{\qquad}$.

B6 **Write 1, 2, 3, . . ., n in a circle. Start at 1 and cross out every second uncrossed number. For which values of n is 1 the last number left?**

The easy step is to realise that, if n is odd (and ≥ 3) then 1 will be crossed out at the start of the second circuit. Hence, for 1 to survive, either $n = 1$ or n must be e∗e∗ (say $n = 2m$).

Suppose $n = 2m$. Then at the start of the second circuit there remain exactly m numbers 1, 3, 5, . . ., $2m - 1$. For 1 to survive next time it is essential that either $m = 1$ (so $n = 2$) or m must be e∗e∗ (say $m = 2p$).

Continuing in this way we see that 1 will be the last uncrossed number if and only if n is a ∗o∗e∗ of ∗∗o.

1994: Section A

A1 What is the angle between the hands of a clock at 9:30?

The angle at the centre is $360°$, so the angle $A°$ subtended at the centre by two successive hour marks must be $\frac{360°}{?} = $ _____ $°$.

At 9:30 the minute hand points directly at _____ while the hour hand is halfway between _____ and _____, so the required angle is $3\frac{1}{2} \times A°$ = _____.

A2 For how many two-digit numbers is the sum of the digits a multiple of 6?

The digits either add to 6 (15, 24, 33, _____, _____, _____) or 12 (_____, _____, _____, _____, _____, _____) or _____ (_____). Hence there are exactly _____ such numbers.

A3 Some shepherds lose two-thirds of their flock and then find four-fifths of these. What fraction of the flock did they have left?

The fraction still lost was $\frac{1}{5}$ of $\frac{2}{3} = $ _____. $\therefore$ _____ of the flock remained.

A4 Two dice numbered 0–5 are thrown. Find the probability that the total is a prime number.

Let the two dice be R (red) and B (blue). Dice R can take six values, dice B can take _____ values, so there are _____ $\times$ _____ = _____ possible outcomes. Possible prime totals are 2, _____, _____ and _____ (only). Look at each one in turn. The total 2 can be obtained as $0 + 2$, $1 + 1$ or $2 + 0$ (three ways); 3 can be obtained as _____, _____, _____, _____ (_____ ways); 5 can be obtained in _____ ways; 7 can be obtained in _____ ways. Hence there are _____ ways in all. So the required probability is $\frac{?}{36}$. (It is not enough just to give the 'answer' 17.)

A5 In rectangle *ABCD*, *AB* = 2 × *BC*; triangle *ABE* overlaps the rectangle and is equilateral; *M* is the midpoint of *BE*. Find ∠*CMB*.

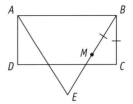

ΔABE is equilateral, so ∠*ABE* = _____°; hence ∠*MBC* = _____°.

$BM = \dfrac{BE}{2} = \dfrac{AB}{2} = BC$; ∴ Δ*BMC* is i*o**e*e*.

Hence ∠BMC = _____.

A6 A normal duck has two legs. A lame duck has one leg. A sitting duck has no legs. Ninety nine ducks have a total of 100 legs. Given that there are half as many sitting ducks as normal ducks and lame ducks put together, find the number of lame ducks.

We use letters to stand for *numbers of things*. Let *N*, *L*, *S* denote the numbers of normal, lame and sitting ducks respectively. Counting ducks gives $N + L + S =$ _____.

Counting legs gives _____ × *N* + *L* = _____. We are told that $S = \dfrac{(N+L)}{2}$, so *N* + *L* = 2*S*. ∴ *N* + *L* + *S* = 3*S* = _____, so *S* = _____, and 100 = 2*N* + *L* = *N* + (*N* + *L*) = *N* + 2*S* = *N* + _____, so *N* = _____. ∴ *L* = _____.

A7 How many different solutions are there to JMO ÷ UK = OK? (Different letters stand for different digits, and no number begins with a zero.)

Translate the division into a *u**i**i*a*io*.

$$\begin{array}{r} \text{O K} \\ \times\ \text{U K} \\ \hline \text{J M O} \end{array}$$

If *K* = _____, or _____, or _____, or _____, then '*O*' = '*K*' which is forbidden.

So we only need check

(a) '*K*' = 2, '*O*' = _____;   (b) '*K*' = 3, '*O*' = _____;   (c) '*K*' = 4, '*O*' = _____;

(d) '*K*' = 7, '*O*' = _____;   (e) '*K*' = 8, '*O*' = _____;   (f) '*K*' = 9, '*O*' = _____.

This looks messy; but the cases are all similar and surprisingly quick once you realise *you must work logically and not guess*. I shall do case (a) and leave the other cases to you.

(a) Suppose '*K*' = 2. Then '*O*' = 4. Now '*OK*' × '*UK*' = 42 × '*U2*' = '*JM4*' <1000, so '*U*'≤ _____; and '*U*' ≠ 2 (since '*K*' = 2). Hence '*U*' = _____ is the only possibility. But then '*M*' = _____, '*J*' = _____, so there is only one possible 'sum' (that is, only one solution to '*OK* × *UK* = *JMO*' with '*K*' = 2). Checking shows that it really works! Now do the others.

A8 **Moses is twice as old as Methuselah was when Methuselah was one-third as old as Moses will be when Moses is as old as Methuselah is now. If the difference in their ages is 666, how old is Methuselah?**

Like many mathematical problems, this is not too hard once you think about it. Let Moses' present age be M years, and Methuselah's present age be m years. Thus, when 'Moses is as old as Methuselah is now' Moses' age will be exactly _____. So the first sentence says only 'Moses is twice as old as Methuselah was when Methuselah was one-third of his present age':

$\therefore M = 2 \times \left(\frac{m}{3}\right)$. Now $m - M = 666$ (given), and $m - M = m - \frac{2m}{3} =$ _____,

$\therefore m =$ _____.

A9 **Find $a + b + c + d$.**

In all geometry problems you must be prepared to put in extra lines to help you to see what is going on. Extend BC to cut the top horizontal line at E and the bottom horizontal line at F. a is an *external* angle of $\triangle AEB$, so $a = u + v$. Similarly $d = x + y$.

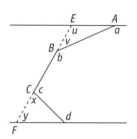

$\therefore a + b + c + d = u + v + b + c + x + y = u + 180 + 180 + y =$ _____
(since $u + y =$ _____).

A10 **A crossnumber is like a crossword except that the answers are numbers, with one digit in each square. What is the sum of all eight digits in this crossnumber?**

Across	1.	Square of a prime
	4.	Prime
	5.	Square

Down	1.	Square of another prime
	2.	Square
	3.	Prime

You should not guess, but must use careful logic. *1 Across* and *1 Down* are both squares of prime numbers *with the same hundreds digit*: there is only one possibility ($17^2 = 2$___, $19^2 = 3$___, $23^2 = 5$___, $29^2 = 8$___, $31^2 = 9$___). Now *5 Across* is a two-digit square, so its first digit cannot be a 9: thus *1 Down* = _____ and *1 Across* = _____. Hence *5 Across* must be _____. So *2 Down* is a square with first digit and last digit both equal to _____; hence *2 Down* = _____. Also *3 Down* is a prime with first digit _____; there is only one prime in the 90s, so *3 Down* = _____. *4 Across* is now determined (and fortunately happens to be prime). Adding the digits gives _____.

1994: Section B

B1 Four quarters of a circle of radius 1 are arranged as shown. Find the area. Explain!

The two bumps on the sides are equal to the two dents top and bottom, so the shape is a rearrangement of a **ua*e. Thus we need to calculate the area of the **ua*e *ABCD*. The *ua*e is made up of two right-angled triangles: *ABC* and *CDA*. Taking the hypotenuse *AC* (equal to the *ia*e*e* of the circle) as 'base', each such triangle has height equal to the *a*iu*. Hence each triangle has area = _____; so the square has area = _____.

B2 (a) Find three prime numbers whose sum is also prime.
    (b) Find three positive integers such that the sum of any two is a square. Can you find other sets of three integers with the same property?

(a) Write out the first few primes: 2, 3, 5, 7, 11, 13, 17, 19, . . . If we choose three primes including 2, the sum will always be e*e* so cannot be prime. If we try the first three *odd primes*, the sum = _____, which is not a prime; trying the first two odd primes (3, 5) and the fourth odd prime (_____) we get sum = _____!

(b) If we were only asked to find *one* set of three integers, we could get by with trial-and-error as in part (a). But the important bit of this question is at the end: 'Can you find other sets of three integers with the same property?' Thus you need a general method for finding sets of three integers 'with the same property'.

Method 1: Take any three *successive* squares – such as 5^2, 6^2, 7^2. The difference $7^2 - 6^2 =$ _____. Choose two integers which differ by this amount, say x and $x +$ _____, and which have sum equal to 5^2 ($\therefore x =$ _____). Then x, $x +$ _____, and $6^2 - x$ are your three numbers (since $x + (x + 13) = 5^2$, $x + (6^2 - x) = 6^2$ and $(x + 13) + (6^2 - x) = 6^2 + 13 = 7^2$).

This method will always work provided two of the squares at the start are o**. (Can you see why?)

Method 2: Suppose you have found one set of three positive integers which work (such as 6, 19, 30), You can then multiply each of these numbers by the same square, say 2^2, to get another set (24, 76, 120) which works. (To demonstrate this, don't slog out the answers to check. Think! The *structure* of the numbers is what matters:

$6 + 19 = 5^2$, $\therefore 6 \times 2^2 + 19 \times 2^2 = (6 + 19)2^2 = 5^2 \times 2^2 = (5 \times 2)^2 = 10^2$.)

Method 3: Suppose the three numbers we want are a, b, c and the squares are x^2, y^2, z^2. Then $a + b = x^2$, $b + c = y^2$, $c + a = z^2$.

$\therefore x^2 + y^2 - z^2 = (a + b) + (b + c) - (c + a) = $ _____ , so $b = \dfrac{x^2 + y^2 - z^2}{2}$.

Similarly $c = $ _____ _____ , $a = $ _____ _____ . If we choose any squares x^2, y^2, z^2, we can calculate a, b, c. The only restriction is that, if a, b, c are to be positive integers, then $x^2 + y^2 + z^2$ must be e∗e∗.

B3 In trapezium $PQRS$, $\angle QRS$ is twice $\angle QPS$, $QR = a$, and $RS = b$. Find PS. Explain!

There are no marks in mathematics (a) for guessing the answer, or (b) for giving the right answer if your reasoning is invalid.

Draw the line RT through R parallel to QP.

Then $\angle QPT = \angle RTS = $ _____ (since $PQ \| TR$).

Now $PQRT$ is a ∗a∗a∗∗e∗o∗∗a∗, so $QR = $ _____ (opposite sides of a parallelogram), and $\angle QPT = \angle$ _____ (opposite angles of a parallelogram). $\angle TRS = \angle QRS - \angle QRT = $ __ $= \angle RTS$.

Hence $\triangle RTS$ is i∗o∗∗e∗e∗, so $b = RS = ST$.

B4 A sequence obeys the rule that, given any two successive terms a, b, the next term is obtained by dividing their product $a.b$ by their sum $a + b$. If the first two terms are $\frac{1}{2}$ and $\frac{1}{3}$, write down the next three terms. What is the tenth term? Explain clearly what is going on, and how you can be sure.

Given two terms a, b, dividing their *sum* by their *product* gives

$$\frac{(a+b)}{(a.b)} = \frac{a}{(ab)} + \frac{b}{(ab)} = \frac{1}{b} + \frac{1}{a}.$$

Hence dividing their *product* ab by their *sum* $a + b$ gives

$\dfrac{1}{\left(\frac{1}{b} + \frac{1}{a}\right)}$. If the first two terms are fractions, $a = \frac{1}{2}$ and $b = \frac{1}{3}$, then $\dfrac{1}{a} = $ _____

and $\dfrac{1}{b} = $ _____ , so the third term is _____ . In general, if two successive terms are $a = \frac{1}{x}$ and $b = \frac{1}{y}$, then $\dfrac{1}{a} = $ _____ and $\dfrac{1}{b} = $ _____ so the next term is $\dfrac{1}{(x+y)}$ Hence the sequence of denominators is just 2, 3, 5, 8, 13, . . ., so the tenth term is $\dfrac{1}{?}$.

B5 Arrange the numbers 1–9 in a 3 by 3 grid so that the total T of all the horizontal and vertical differences between adjacent squares is as large as possible. Prove that no other arrangement could give a larger total T.

Despite this being far the hardest question, it was the one question almost all candidates, quite wrongly, thought they could do! One mistake was so widespread that it must be dealt with before we can begin the outline solution. (Indeed, the mistake is so common that it even has a name: it is called the 'greedy' assumption, and you will soon understand why.)

Trial-and-error should give you a good idea what the largest possible total T is. If you think carefully, it should also give you a clear idea how the numbers have to be arranged. Explaining clearly and correctly *why* no other arrangement can give a larger total is much, much harder.

It may *seem* sensible to put the 9 (or the 1) in the centre square. However, it is simply not acceptable in mathematics to say

> 'I think this is the largest because the 9 in the middle has lots of small numbers near it so this gives lots of big differences.'

This is not a proof. If we put the 9 in the middle we can make four differences large, but we make the other eight differences *smaller* than they could be. We then lose control of the total T of all the differences: grabbing as much as we can in the middle *leaves less to go round elsewhere*. In this problem no correct proof can start by focusing on the centre square.

Whenever you are experimenting in a problem (to find the *largest*, or *smallest*, or best *overall* arrangement), you are free to use any approach you like in rough. But when you come to *prove* that what you *think* is the best really is the best, you must

> never assume that if you grab the best possible start . . .
> you will automatically get the best possible overall result.

To win a marathon it is not always wise to run the first mile at top speed! More important, our concern is not just with guessing the *answer* (perhaps this 'greedy' approach really does give the best overall total T in this case), but with *reasons* (how can we be sure that no other arrangement could possibly do better?).

I hope you now understand why you must avoid simply being 'greedy' on behalf of the 9. Instead you must try to think about *all* the numbers together. If you look carefully at what you *think* is the best possible arrangement (there are in fact *lots* of them, but your own favourite arrangement will do), you should notice something more interesting than just the way numbers are arranged around the centre square. This could give you the key idea in the proof. But before we begin you must

- clear your mind,

- forget what you think is the best arrangement, and

- use logic.

You are now ready to begin the solution! The only pairs that contribute to the total T are pairs with a horizontal or a vertical difference. *If you colour the squares black and white*, then each such pair involves one white square and one black. Hence the largest possible total T must arise when the nine numbers 1–9 are split into five white and four black numbers with the differences between whites and blacks being as large as possible. To make the differences as big as possible you want the whites to be as large as possible and the blacks as small as possible, or the other way round.

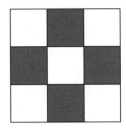

Hence *either* (a) the five whites are 5, 6, 7, 8, 9 and the four blacks are 1, 2, 3, 4, *or* (b) the five whites are 1, 2, 3, 4, 5 and the four blacks are 6, 7, 8, 9.

Notice that whenever you have an arrangement of the first kind with total T, then swapping 1 and 9, 2 and 8, 3 and 7, 4 and 6 changes it into an arrangement of the second kind *with the same total T*. In trying to find the largest possible total T you can therefore concentrate on arrangements of the first kind. Thus you may assume that 1, 2, 3, 4 go on black squares and that 5, 6, 7, 8, 9 go on white squares.

You have still not proved that 9 has to go in the middle square. Suppose the 9 is *not* in the centre. Then it must be on a corner square, with some other number x in the centre. Let a, b be the two black numbers adjacent to both 9 and x. If you swap 9 and x, the differences with a and b which contribute to the total T are unchanged. But since $9 \geq x$, the differences with c, d (≤ 4) increase. Hence for the largest total T, 9 must be in the centre.

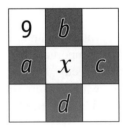

It remains to arrange 5, 6, 7, 8 on the white squares and 1, 2, 3, 4 on the black squares to give the largest total T. I leave you to provide a similar argument to explain why all possible arrangements *give the same total T*.

B6 Find the fraction of the rectangle $ABCD$ in problem **1994 A5** that is covered by triangle ABE.

Let $AB = 2$, $BC = 1$. Suppose AE and BE cut DC at X and Y respectively. Then $\angle DAE =$ _____,

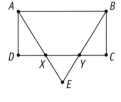

so $DX = \dfrac{DX}{AD} = \tan \angle DAE = \dfrac{1}{\sqrt{3}}$ (exactly!).

$\therefore$ area $(\triangle ADX) = \dfrac{DX.AD}{2} = \dfrac{1}{2\sqrt{3}} =$ area $(\triangle BCY)$;

so area $(ABYX) = 2 - \dfrac{1}{\sqrt{3}}$.

$\therefore$ fraction of rectangle $ABCD$ covered $= \dfrac{2 - \dfrac{1}{\sqrt{3}}}{2} = 1 - \dfrac{1}{2\sqrt{3}}$.

1993: Section A

A1 Start with 1993 and multiply the digits to get a new number. Repeat until you get a single digit.

$1993 \rightarrow 1 \times 9 \times 9 \times 3 =$ _____ $\rightarrow 2 \times 4 \times 3 =$ _____ $\rightarrow 2 \times 4 = 8$.

A2 A rectangle is cut into four pieces. The areas of three pieces are given. Find the area of the original rectangle.

	y	z
a	6	10
b	9	?

Let the four boxes have measurements $a \times y$, $a \times z$, $b \times y$, $b \times z$.

Then $6 : 9 = (a \times y) : (b \times y) = a : b = (a \times z) : (b \times z) = 10 : ?$;

$\therefore ? = 15$, area $= 40$.

A3 Evaluate $0.123\,451\,234\,512\,3\,\ldots + 0.987\,659\,876\,5598\,7\,\ldots$ exactly as a fraction.

Each column in the sum gives the answer '0', carry '1'. Thus the answer as a *decimal* is $1.111\,111\,\ldots$ (forever). We have to write this *as a fraction.* You should *know* that $0.111\,111\,\ldots$ (forever) is the decimal for _____. But, if you did not, then you should certainly have known that $0.333\,333\,\ldots$ (forever) is the decimal for _____, and $0.111\,111\,\ldots$ (forever) is exactly one-third of this. So $1.111\,111\,\ldots$ (forever) = _____.

$$+\begin{array}{l}0.123\,451\,234\,512\,345\,123\ldots\\ 0.987\,659\,876\,598\,765\,987\ldots\end{array}$$

(**Question:** What is '$0.999\,999\,\ldots$ (forever)' equal to?)

A4 Three ropes of lengths **8 m, 9 m, 10 m** are laid on the ground as shown. *AB* is the longest arc. How long is it?

Each rope covers *two* arcs; so arc(AB) + arc(BC), arc(BC) + arc(CA), arc(CA) + arc(AB) are equal to 8, 9, 10 in some order. Since arc(AB) is the longest arc, the two ropes of the form 'arc(AB)+ ???' must be the two longest ropes, and the rope 'arc(BC) + arc(CA)' must be the shortest. Thus $BC + CA = $ _____; and $AB + BC$, $CA + AB$ equal _____, _____ in some order. Hence $19 = AB + BC + CA + AB = 2 \times AB + (BC + CA) = 2 \times AB + $ _____.
∴ arc(AB) = 5.5 m.

A5 Two numbers have difference, sum, and product in the ratio **1 : 4 : 15**. What are they?

Let the numbers be a and b. Then $a - b : a + b : ab = 1 : 4 : 15$, so $\frac{(a+b)}{(a-b)} = \frac{4}{1}$;
∴ $5b = 3a$. Hence $\frac{4}{15} = \frac{(a+b)}{ab} = \frac{3(a+b)}{3ab} = \frac{8b}{5b^2} = \frac{8}{5b}$.
∴ $b = $ _____, and $a = $ _____.

A6 The radius of the two smallest circles is one-sixth that of the largest circle. The radius of the middle-sized circle is double that of the small circles. What fraction of the large circle is shaded?

Let the radius of the smallest circles be r. Then the middle-sized circle has radius $2r$ and the large circle has radius $6r$. Thus the shaded area is $\pi(6r)^2 - \pi(2r)^2 - 2 \times \pi r^2 = \pi.$ _____ r^2,
so the fraction shaded is $\frac{\pi.30r^2}{\pi.(6r)^2} = $ _____.

A7 In a sequence of points, the point (x,y) is followed by $(x + 2y, 2x - y)$. If the first point is (a,b), what is the fifth point?

$$(x, y) \rightarrow (x', y') = (x + 2y, 2x - y)$$
$$\rightarrow (x' + 2y', 2x' - y') = ((x + 2y) + 2(2x - y), 2(x + 2y) - (2x - y))$$
$$= (5x, 5y).$$

Thus if the first point of the sequence is (a, b) the *third* point will be $(5a, 5b)$. We have just shown that, *whenever* we do two steps, the two coordinates are simply multiplied by 5. Thus

$$(a, b) \rightarrow \ldots \rightarrow (5a, 5b) \rightarrow \ldots \rightarrow (25a, 25b).$$

1st point   3rd point   5th point

A8 *ABCDEFGH* is a cube of side 3. *X* is one-third of the way along *AB*, *Y* is one-third of the way along *GH*, and *Z* is two-thirds of the way down *DE*. Find the area of triangle *XYZ*.

If *X* is one-third of the way along *AB* and *Y* is one-third of the way along *GH*, then $XG^2 = 2^2 + 3^2$, so $XY^2 = $ _____. Similarly if *Z* is two-thirds of the way down *DE*, then $YZ^2 = $ _____, and $ZX^2 = $ _____. Hence *XYZ* is equilateral with sides of length $\sqrt{14}$. For the area we need the height: draw the perpendicular *XM* from *X* to the midpoint *M* of *YZ*; then

$$XM^2 = XY^2 - YM^2 = (\sqrt{14})^2 - \left(\frac{\sqrt{14}}{2}\right)^2 = \underline{\quad}.$$
$$\therefore XM = \frac{\sqrt{3 \times 14}}{2}, \text{ area } (\triangle XYZ) = \frac{7}{2}\sqrt{3}.$$

A9 At what time is the angle between the hands of a clock exactly 170°?

170° is just 10° less than 180°, so try to get the hands pointing *almost* in opposite directions. This is easiest if one hand points *exactly* at an hour mark.

The angle between two successive hour marks is _____°, so the hour hand moves 10° in _____ minutes. This suggests trying '20 past _____' or '20 to _____'.

There are lots of other answers, though they are harder to find. You might like to try to find them all.

A10 **In how many different ways can one pay 20p using standard British coins?**

This is a toughie. We can

(A) use a 20p coin (one way); or (B) use no 20p coins (??? ways).

Let us look at (B) more closely. We may use

(B1) two 10ps (one way), or (B2) one 10p (? ways),
or (B3) no 10ps (?? ways).

(B2) If we use only one 10p coin, we have to make 10p using only 5ps, 2ps, 1ps (*two* 5ps – **one way**; one 5p – **three ways**; no 5ps – **six ways**), making ten ways altogether.

(B3) If we use no 10p coins, we have to make 20p using only 5ps, 2ps, 1ps (four 5ps – **one way**; three 5ps – **three ways**; two 5ps – **six ways**; one 5p – **eight ways**; no 5ps – **eleven ways**), making _____ ways altogether.

Adding all these possibilities then gives _____ ways.

1993: Section B

B1 **Place 1–8 at vertices of a cube with each face having the same sum. What do you notice about the two numbers at *A* and *B* and the two numbers at *C* and *D*? Explain.**

It is almost impossible to fail to label the cube in the required way: there are lots of different ways of doing it. But all of them have $A + B = C + D$. Why? You have to give a mathematical reason which is completely general. In particular, your reasons must not depend on your particular labelling.

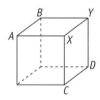

Proof: In any labelling where each face has the same sum, the faces *ABYX* and *CDYX* must have the same sum: that is, $A + B + X + Y = C + D + X + Y$. Hence $A + B = C + D$.

B2 31.3.93 is an 'interesting' date since $31 \times 3 = 93$. If all dates are written like this, how many years in the twentieth century contain no interesting dates at all?

31.3.93 is an interesting date, since $31 \times 3 = 93$. We have to count years which can't be factorised as 'date × month number'.

Years up to (19)31 all have interesting dates in the month of _____. Even years up to (19)56 have interesting dates in the month of _____. Years ≤ 93 with a factor of 3, lead to interesting dates in March; and $96 = 24 \times 4$, $99 = 9 \times 11$, so 1996 and 1999 also have interesting dates; hence every year '*ab*' which is a multiple of 3 contains at least one interesting date. Every year which has a factor of 4 has an interesting date in April (in fact before 25 April). Similarly, any year '*ab*' which has a factor of 5 (or 6, 7, 8, 9, 10, 11, or 12) has an interesting date in May (or June, July, August, September, October, November, or December respectively). Thus we only have to worry about two sorts of year '*ab*':

(i) years '*ab*' > 31 which have no factors at all (that is, the remaining prime numbers '*ab*' < 100: _____, _____, _____, _____, _____, _____, _____, _____, _____, _____, _____, _____, _____, _____);

and

(ii) even years '*ab*' > 56 which are not multiples of 3, 4, 5, 6, 7, 8, 9, 10, 11, or 12 (that is, the numbers of the form '$2 \times p$' where p is a prime number ≥ 29: _____, _____, _____, _____, _____, _____).

We then only have to decide which of 1900 and 2000 belongs to the twentieth century.

B3 (a) A 2 by 2 square has semicircles drawn on each edge as shown. The overlaps create four shaded 'petals'. Find the shaded area.

(b) A regular hexagon with sides of length 2 has semicircles drawn on each side (pointing inwards as before). The overlaps create six 'petals'. Find the total area of the six 'petals'.

(a) The four semicircles cover the whole square, covering each petal twice. Hence the sum of the areas of the four semicircles gives the area of the square plus the shaded area:

$$4 \times \left(\frac{\pi}{2}\right) = 2 \times 2 + (4 \text{ petals}) \quad \therefore \text{ area(shaded petals)} = 2\pi - 4.$$

85

(b) The method used in (a) above does not generalise to (b), since the six semicircles in (b) don't cover the whole hexagon: the six semicircles do not go through the centre of the hexagon!

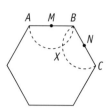

Let AB and BC be two sides of the hexagon, with midpoints M and N.

Let the semicircles on AB and on BC meet at X.

Then $MB = BN = NX = XM = 1$, so $MBNX$ is a **o**u*.

Since $\angle MBN = $ _____°, we know that $\angle BNX = $ _____°.

Thus the sector NBX is exactly one-*i*** of a circle, so has area $= \frac{\pi \cdot 1^2}{6}$.

Similarly $\angle BMX = $ _____°, so the sector MBX has area $\frac{\pi}{6}$.

Thus $2 \times \left(\frac{\pi}{6}\right) = $ area(rhombus $MBNX$) + area('petal BX'). We must calculate the area of the rhombus $MBNX$, which has base $NX = 1$ and height h equal to the distance between NX and MB. Hence h is the height of the equilateral triangle BNX, so $h = \sqrt{(1^2 - (\frac{1}{2})^2)} = \frac{\sqrt{3}}{2}$;

$\therefore$ area('petal BX') $= \frac{\pi}{3} - \left(1 \times \frac{\sqrt{3}}{2}\right)$, so area(6 petals) $= 2\pi - 3\sqrt{3}$.

B4 Does there exist a four-digit perfect square 'aabb'?

Suppose $N^2 = $ '$aabb$' is a four-digit square (so a and b are digits ≤ 9). Clearly $N \geq 32$ and $N \leq 99$. Also $N^2 = a \times 1100 + b \times 11 = 11(100a + b)$, so N^2 is a multiple of 11. But then N must itself be a multiple of 11, so we only have to try $N = 99, 88, 77, 66, 55, 44, 33$. Hence $N = $ _____.

Another approach is to observe that we want $100a + b = $ '$a0b$' to be 11 times a square; so we only need to look at multiples of 11 whose tens digits is 0: $209 = 11 \times 19$, $308 = $ _____, $407 = $ _____, $506 = $ _____, $605 = $ _____, $704 = $ _____, $803 = $ _____, $902 = $ _____.

B5 (a) **Which pairs of numbers a, b satisfy $a + b = a \times b$?**

(b) **Can you find three numbers a, b, c such that $a + b + c = a \times b \times c$? Four numbers? Five? . . .**

(a) The example $2 + 2 = 2 \times 2$ shows that repeated digits are allowed!

Suppose $a + b = a \times b$. Then a cannot be 1 (since $b + 1 \neq b \times 1$). Adding $-b$ to both sides of $a + b = ab$ we get $b(a - 1) = a$, so $b = \frac{a}{(a-1)}$. Thus the only possible pairs are of the form a, $b = \frac{a}{(a-1)}$ with $a \neq 1$.

Conversely, when a is any number different from 1, the pair a, $b = \frac{a}{(a-1)}$ has the desired property. (Examples: $a = 3$, $b = \frac{3}{2}$; or $a = 4$, $b = \frac{4}{3}$; or $a = \pi$, $b = \frac{\pi}{(\pi-1)}$.)

(b) For three numbers you should very quickly find $1 + 2 + 3 = 1 \times 2 \times 3$. A little algebra as in part (a) then gives the family of triples 1, a, $\frac{(a+1)}{(a-1)}$.

For four numbers you may have to experiment a bit before finding $1, 1, 2, 4$ (and the corresponding infinite family $1, 1, a, \frac{(a+2)}{(a-1)}$).

At this stage you should realise that to solve $a + b + c = abc$ you can choose the first two numbers a, b in any way at all (provided their product ab is not equal to 1), and that the third number c is then determined by $c(ab - 1) = a + b$, so $c = \frac{(a+b)}{(ab-1)}$.

In general to find n numbers whose sum is equal to their product, you can choose the first $n - 1$ numbers in any way at all (provided their product is not equal to 1), and the last number is then determined.

Hence for longer lists the really interesting question is to find lists of n *whole* numbers with the 'sum = product' property.

One example is the list $1, 1, \ldots, 1, 2, n$ containing $(n - 2)$ 1s, one 2 and one n; this generalises the earlier examples $2, 2$ (no 1s, two 2s), $1, 2, 3$ (one 1, one 2, one 3) and $1, 1, 2, 4$. Are there any other lists of n whole numbers that work?

(Answers consisting only of 0s, such as $0 + 0 + 0 + 0 = 0.0.0.0$, are correct, but not very interesting. Answers like $1 + (-1) + 0 + 0 = 1.(-1).0.0$ are only slightly better.)

B6 **Find the area of the overlap of $AB'CD'$ and $A'BC'D$ as a fraction of $ABCD$.**

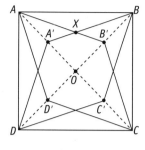

A' is the midpoint of OA, and B' is the midpoint of BO.

$\therefore A'B' = \dfrac{AB}{2}$ and $A'B'$ is parallel to AB.

Hence area$(A'B'C'D') = \dfrac{\text{area}(ABCD)}{4}$.

Let AB' and $A'B$ meet at X.

Then triangles $A'B'X$ and BAX are similar (since $\angle A'XB' = \angle BXA$ – vertically opposite; $\angle A'B'X = \angle BAX$ – alternate angles);

$\therefore$ corresponding sides are in the ratio $A'B' : AB = 1 : 2$.

Hence

$$\text{area } (A'B'X) = \frac{\text{area}(BAX)}{2^2}, \text{ and } XA : XB' = 2 : 1;$$
$$\therefore \text{area}(A'B'X) = \frac{\text{area}(AXA')}{2} = \left(\frac{1}{9}\right) \times \text{area}(ABB'A') = \left(\frac{1}{48}\right) \times \text{area}(ABCD).$$

Adding $A'B'C'D'$ and the four triangles like $A'B'X$ we see that, as a fraction of the square $ABCD$, the overlap covers $(\frac{1}{4}) + 4 \times (\frac{1}{48}) = \frac{1}{3}$.

(There are lots of other proofs. For example, $AA' = A'O$; $\therefore$ area$(A'OX) =$ area$(AA'X)$, and $BB' = OB'$; $\therefore$ area$(B'BA) =$ area$(OB'A) = 3 \times$ area$(A'OX)$, so area$(OA'XB') = \frac{1}{3}$ area(OAB).)

1992: Section A

A1 **Which multiple of 11 is nearest to 1000?**

Note that 99 is a multiple of 11, but 999 is *not* (Why not?).

$1000 = 11 \times 90 + 10 = 11 \times 91 - 1$, so $11 \times 91 = 1001$ is the nearest multiple of 11.

A2 **A cuboid has volume $\frac{1}{4}$ cm^3, height $\frac{2}{3}$ cm, depth $\frac{1}{2}$ cm. What is its width?**

$\frac{1}{2} \times \frac{2}{3} \times$ width $= \frac{1}{4}$; $\therefore$ width $=$ ___.

(**Note:** When solving $\frac{1}{2} \times \frac{2}{3} \times ? = \frac{1}{4}$, you should not be satisfied with the answer $\frac{6}{8}$.)

A3 **What is the smallest number which is the sum of two primes in two ways?**

The small prime numbers are 2, 3, 5, 7, 11, 13, 17, . . . If an odd number n is the sum of two prime numbers, one must be even and the other odd; the only even prime is 2, so the odd prime must be $n - 2$. In particular, there is at most one way of writing an odd number as the sum of two primes.

Hence the smallest number which can be written as the sum of two prime numbers in *two* different ways must be e∗e∗. If we try each even number in turn, we find $8 = 3 + 5$, $10 = 3 + 7$, $12 = 5 + 7$, $14 = 3 + 11$, $16 = 3 + 13 = $ _____ .

(**Note:** 1 is not a prime number. Find out why not.)

A4 **On holiday I always wear pants, shorts, T-shirt and sunglasses. I have to put on the T-shirt before the sunglasses, and the pants before the shorts. Each day I dress in a different order. For how long can I keep this up?**

To get dressed I put on four items of clothing in order; item 1, item 2, item 3, item 4. Thus I have to decide which item to put on in each of the four positions in this sequence. If I choose two of these positions for *pants* and *shorts* (in that order), the other two have to be *T-shirt* and *sunglasses* (in that order). Since there are exactly _____ ways of choosing the two positions for *pants* and *shorts*, I can keep it up for exactly _____ days.

A5 **The first term is $\frac{3}{8}$; if x is any term, the next is $\frac{(1-x)}{(1+x)}$. What is the eighth term?**

The second term is $\dfrac{(1 - \frac{3}{8})}{(1 + \frac{3}{8})} = \dfrac{(\frac{5}{8})}{(\frac{11}{8})} = \frac{5}{11}$. The third term is then the same as the first term! Thus the fourth term must be _____ (the same as the ∗e∗o∗∗ term), and so on. Hence the eighth term must be _____ .

A6 **Four pipes of diameter 1 m are tied in a 'square' shape by a band. How long is the band?**

The four curved sections are *quarter circles*, so together make up a whole circle of diameter 1 m; thus the curved bits have total length exactly _____ . Each of the four straight bits is equal to two radii, and so has length exactly _____ . Thus the total length is exactly _____ .

A7 **In question A6 what is the cross-sectional area of the hole between the four pipes?**

Joining the centres of the four pipes produces a square with side length 1 m, and hence area _____ m^2. To calculate the shaded area we must subtract the four quarter circles: these fit together to make a complete circle of radius $\frac{1}{2}$ m, so their total area is $\pi(\frac{1}{2})^2$. Thus the shaded area is equal to _____ m^2.

A8 **My children are all at school and the product of their ages is 60 060. How many children do I have?**

$$60\,060 = 2 \times 30\,030 = \ldots = 2 \times 2 \times 3 \times 5 \times 7 \times 11 \times 13.$$

Each child's age lies between 5 and 18, so two of the children must be 11 and 13, while the other ages multiplied together give $2 \times 2 \times 3 \times 5 \times 7$.

This does not determine their ages (there are several different solutions); but it does tell you how many children I have, namely _____.

A9 **If I stand with one foot each side of the Equator, how fast am I moving?**

The circumference rotates round once in 24 hours; thus I move $2\pi.(6500)$ km in 24 hours, or $\dfrac{2\pi.6500}{24}$ km per hour. $\dfrac{2\pi.6500}{24} = \dfrac{\pi.6500}{12} = \dfrac{\pi.3250}{6} = \dfrac{\pi.1625}{3}$ which is slightly less than 542π. I would thus be whizzed round at approximately 1700 km per hour.

A10 **29/2/92 is palindromic. How many palindromic dates are there between 1910 and 1999?**

The question refers to 29/2/92, *not* 29/02/92. This indicates that single digit numbers like '7' should *not* be written '07'.

'*Between 1910 and 1999*' is less clear: it may, or may not, include 1910. But the previous remark shows that there are *no palindromic dates in 1910* (Why not?), so it does not matter!

For a year 19*ab* to have a palindromic date ?/?/*ab*, the reverse *ba* must be a possible date in some month, so *b* must be ≤_____, and cannot be 0. Thus in the first decade there are just three possible years (19)1__, (19)1__, (19)1__; while in every subsequent decade there are just two possible years (ending in _____ or _____). Thus between 1910 and 1999 there are precisely $3 + (8 \times 2)$ years with palindromic dates.

All that remains is to see how many ways there are of filling in the month number, and to check that each gives rise to a possible date. The only non-palindromic month numbers are October (10) and December (12). Hence, with the exception of the year 1913 (where we are restricted to palindromic months with 31 days), each possible year has exactly _____ palindromic dates (this depends on the fact that 1992 was a *ea* year!). So the total number of palindromic dates between 1910 and 1999 is $(18 \times 10) + 5$.

1992: Section B

B1 Can the difference between 'ab' and its reverse 'ba' ever be a prime number?

Method 1: *First a digression.* Suppose we have a two-digit number 'xy' whose tens digit x and units digit y have sum $x + y = 9$; then our number 'xy' $= 10x + y = 9x + (x + y) = 9x + 9$ is always a multiple of 9.

Now back to the problem. Suppose $a > b$. Then 'ab' – 'ba' has units digit $10 + b - a$ and tens digit $a - b - 1$. The sum of these two digits is $10 + b - a + a - b - 1 =$ _____, so the digression above shows that the difference 'ab' – 'ba' is always a multiple of 9, and so can never be prime number.

Method 2: The two-digit number 'ab' is really $10a + b$. The difference between 'ab' and its reverse 'ba' is $(10a + b) - (10b + a) = 10a - a + b - 10b$ $= 9(a - b)$, which is always a multiple of __ so can never be a **i*e *u**e*.

B2 $ABCDEFGH$ is a regular octagon. How big is $\angle ADG$?

Method 1: Let DE and GF meet at Z.

$\angle ZEF$ and $\angle ZFE$ are external angles of a regular octagon, so both equal __.

$\therefore \triangle ZEF$ is i*o**e*e*, so ZE and ZF must be e*ua*.

Since $ABCDEFGH$ is regular, the sides ED and FG are e*ua*;

$\therefore ZD$ and ZG are e*ua*, so $\triangle ZDG$ is i*o**e*e*.

$\therefore \angle ZDG$ and $\angle ZGD$ are both equal to _____. Hence $\angle GDE =$ _____.

If we extend AB and DC to meet at Y, we get in the same way $\angle CDA =$ _____.

Thus $\angle ADG = \angle CDE - \angle CDA - \angle GDE = 135° - 45° - 45° = 45°$.

Method 2: AD is parallel to BC, and DG is parallel to HC and AB.

$\angle ABC = 135°$, so $\angle ADG = \angle BCH = 45°$.

B3 **A sequence begins 1, 1, . . . Each new term is obtained by adding the inverses of the two previous terms and then taking the inverse of the answer. Find the eighth term and explain, with proof, how the sequence continues.**

Suppose two successive terms are $\frac{1}{x}$ and $\frac{1}{y}$. The next term is obtained by adding their inverses $\left(\dfrac{1}{\left(\frac{1}{x}\right)} + \dfrac{1}{\left(\frac{1}{y}\right)} = \underline{\qquad} \right)$, and then taking the inverse of

the answer to get $\dfrac{1}{(x+y)}$. Thus the sequence goes $\frac{1}{1}, \frac{1}{1}, \frac{1}{2}, \frac{1}{3}, \frac{1}{5}, \frac{1}{8}, \ldots$ whose

terms are just the 'inverses' of the terms of the familiar *Fibonacci* sequence.

B4 **Find the surface area of a cube which just fits in a sphere of radius 1 cm.**

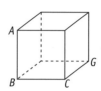

Let the cube have edges of length x cm. Then each face has area x^2 cm^2, so the cube has surface area $6x^2$ cm^2.

All we have to do is to find x.

If the cube just fits inside a sphere, the centre of the sphere will be at the centre of the cube, with the eight corners of the cube touching the sphere. Thus AG is a diameter of the sphere and so has length $\underline{\qquad}$. Hence $AG^2 = \underline{\qquad}$.

Applying Pythagoras' theorem to the two right-angled triangles ACG and ABC we get $AG^2 = AC^2 + CG^2 = AC^2 + x^2 = (AB^2 + BC^2) + x^2$. Hence $4 = AG^2 = 3x^2$ so $x = \underline{\ \ }$, and the surface area of the cube is $6x^2 = \underline{\qquad}$.

(**Note:** Remember we want *exact* answers.)

B5 **(a) Which primes can be expressed as the difference of two squares?**
(b) Which primes can be so expressed in two or more different ways?

(a) Since the gaps between consecutive squares increase $(1, 3, 5, 7, 9, \ldots)$ it is impossible to express the prime 2 as a difference of two squares.

Claim: All *odd* primes p can be expressed as a difference of two squares.

Proof: $(n + 1)^2 = n^2 + (2n + 1)$; so if we choose the integer n so that $2n + 1 = p$, then p is equal to the difference $(n + 1)^2 - n^2$.

(b) *Claim:* No primes can be so expressed in more than one way. (Hence, by the previous part, every odd prime can be expressed in exactly one way.)

Proof: Suppose p is a prime and $p = a^2 - b^2$ for some integers a and b. Then $p = a^2 - b^2 = (a - b)(a + b)$.

But p is a prime number, so it has no factors other than 1 and itself. Moreover, since $a > b$, the second bracket is bigger than the first.

∴ $a - b =$ _____, and $a + b =$ _____. Hence $a =$ _____ and $b =$ _____, so there is only one way of writing p as the difference of two squares.

B6 Find the area of the shaded region.

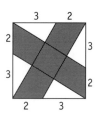

Method 1: The large square has area $S =$ _____. If we remove the shaded cross, then the four white triangles slide together to make a square of side 3 with a hole H in the middle. If we can find the area H of the hole, then the area of the shaded cross will be

$$S - (3^2 - H) = 16 + H.$$

The four white triangles have the same angles as, and so are *similar* to, each of the large right-angled triangles in the original diagram, with sides of length 3, 5, and _____. Now the small white triangles have hypotenuse of known length = _____, so we can use ratios to work out the lengths x, y of the other two sides:

$$x : 3 = 3 : \sqrt{34} = y : 5.$$

Hence the hole has side $y - x =$ _____, so has area $H =$ _____.

Thus the shaded region has area _____.

Method 2: Each sloping shaded strip is a parallelogram with base _____ and height _____. Thus the shaded region has area $10 + 10 -$ (area of the central square). Now

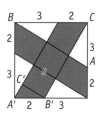

$$AB^2 = AC^2 + BC^2, \text{ so } AB = \underline{\hspace{1cm}}$$
(no approximations please!).

$\triangle ABC$ and $\triangle A'B'C'$ are *i*i*a*; ∴ $\dfrac{A'B'}{AB} = \dfrac{B'C'}{BC}$, so $\dfrac{2}{\sqrt{34}} = \dfrac{B'C'}{5}$.

∴ $s = B'C' =$ _____, hence the central square has area $=$ _____, so the complete shaded region has area $20 -$ _____ $=$ _____.

1991: Section A

A1 **What is the largest prime factor of 1991?**

1991 = 11 × 181 and both 11 and 181 are prime, so the largest prime factor is **181**.

A2 **If Anne earns £$\frac{5}{6}$ per $\frac{4}{5}$ hour and Ben earns £$\frac{7}{8}$ per $\frac{6}{7}$ hour, how long must Ann and Ben work (as a team) to earn £66?**

Ann receives (£$\frac{5}{6}$) ÷ $\frac{4}{5}$ = £$\frac{25}{24}$ per hour, and Ben receives (£$\frac{7}{8}$) ÷ $\frac{6}{7}$ = £$\frac{49}{48}$ per hour. So the team receives £$\frac{99}{48}$ = £$\frac{33}{16}$ per hour. For H hours' work the team receives £$\frac{33}{16}$ × H. So we must solve $\frac{33}{16}$ × H = 66, that is, H = _____.

A3 **In the square $ABCD$, M bisects BC and N bisects AD. The circle centre N through M cuts CD at P. Find $\angle PNM$.**

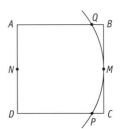

Let the circle centre N through M meet AB at Q. Then $NP = NM = NQ = PQ$, so triangle NPQ is equilateral. Hence angle $PNM = 30°$.

A4 **Find a number less than 100 which increases by 20% when its digits are reversed.**

Let the number be 'ab' = 10 × a + b. We want to choose a, b so that 'ba' is 20% larger than 'ab'; that is $(10 × b + a) = \frac{6}{5}(10 × a + b)$. Solving this equation we get $\frac{44b}{5} = 11a$, so $4b = 5a$. Since a and b have to be (small) whole numbers, the only solution is $a =$ _____, $b =$ _____, so the starting number was _____.

A5 **Each semicircle has radius 1 cm. Find the total area enclosed.**

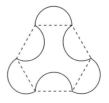

Each semicircular bump can be cut off and used to fill the opposite dent. Thus we must calculate the area of a regular hexagon with sides of length 2 cm. This is made up of six identical equilateral triangles. If we cut one of these triangles in half and use Pythagoras' theorem, we see that it has height $\sqrt{3}$ cm and so has area ($\frac{1}{2}$ × 2 × $\sqrt{3}$) cm².

Thus the regular hexagon has area _____ cm².

A6 Razia broke her necklace. She found one-third of the beads on the floor, one-quarter in her pocket, one-fifth down the side of the sofa, while one-sixth remained on the string; six beads were never found. How many beads were there to start with?

Let the number of beads originally on the necklace be b.

Then $\dfrac{b}{3} + \dfrac{b}{4} + \dfrac{b}{5} + \dfrac{b}{6} + 6 = b$. Solving gives $b = \mathbf{120}$.

A7 The points A, B, C, D, E and F are at the 12, 2, 3, 6, 8 and 9 o'clock hour marks on a clockface. Find the ratio of the area of $ABDE$ to the area of $ACDF$.

Since AD is a diameter of the circle, both $ABDE$ and $ACDF$ are rectangles. Changing scale does not affect the ratio of the areas of these rectangles so we suppose the clockface has radius 2. Then $AB = OA = 2$. Let G be the 4 o'clock mark and let OG and BD meet at P. Then $OP = 1$ (Why?), so in triangle BPO we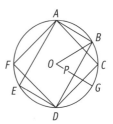
have $BP = \sqrt{3}$, $BD = 2\sqrt{3}$. Hence $ABDE$ has area $2 \times 2\sqrt{3}$. In triangle ACO we have $AO = OC = 2$, so $AC = 2\sqrt{2}$. Similarly $CD = 2\sqrt{2}$. Thus $ACDF$ has area $2\sqrt{2} \times 2\sqrt{2}$. Thus the required ratio is $4\sqrt{3} : 8 = \sqrt{3} : 2$.

A8 The first two terms of a sequence are a and b. Each new term is obtained by dividing the previous term by the one before that. What is the eighth term in the sequence?

Simplifying as we go we see that the sequence goes:

a, b, $\dfrac{b}{a}$, $\dfrac{b}{a} \div b = \dfrac{1}{a}$, $\dfrac{1}{a} \div \dfrac{b}{a} = \dfrac{1}{b}$, $\dfrac{1}{b} \div \dfrac{1}{a} = \dfrac{a}{b}$,

$\dfrac{a}{b} \div \dfrac{1}{b} = a$, $a \div \dfrac{a}{b} = b$.

A9 A net for a pyramid has a square base of side length $10\,\text{cm}$ with an equilateral triangle on each side of the square. What will be the height of the pyramid after it has been made?

The apex of the pyramid, the centre of the base, and a corner of the base form a right-angled triangle; $\therefore h^2 = 10^2 - (\sqrt{50})^2 = 50$, so $h = \sqrt{50} = 5\sqrt{2}$.

A10 **In how many ways can 105 equal the sum of consecutive positive integers?**

If n consecutive numbers add to 105, their average will be $\frac{105}{n}$. If n is odd, this average must be the middle number (and so must be a whole number); if n is even, it must be midway between the two middle numbers (and so must be 'some whole number plus a half'). $\frac{105}{2} = 52.5$, so $105 = 52 + 53$; $\frac{105}{3} = 35$, so $105 = 34 + 35 + 36$; and so on down to $\frac{105}{15} = 7$, at which point we can no longer get 15 consecutive *positive* integers with average $= 7$. The values of n which do work are $n = 2, 3, 5, 6, 7, 10, 14$; the others don't work because $\frac{105}{4} = 26\frac{1}{4}$, $\frac{105}{8} = 13\frac{1}{8}$, $\frac{105}{9} = 11\frac{2}{3}$, $\frac{105}{11} = 9\frac{6}{11}$, $\frac{105}{12} = 8\frac{3}{4}$, $\frac{105}{13} = \underline{\hspace{2cm}}$.

1991: Section B

B1 **Find the shortest and longest gaps between successive palindromic years.**

1111 is a palindrome, so the last palindrone occurred after the year 1000 and so has first and last digits equal to 1. The middle two digits must be equal and less than 9. Thus 1881 was the last palindromic year before 1991.

If single-digit years count as palindromes, then the shortest gap is one year – for example, between AD 1 and AD 2. Otherwise a one-year gap will always turn a palindrome into a non-palindrome (adding 1 either changes the last digit only, which can no longer be equal to the first digit, or else the last digit was a 9 and changes to a 0, which cannot then be equal to the first digit), and so the shortest gap is two years – for example, the gap between AD 9 and AD 11, or between AD 99 and AD 101.

Consider a palindromic year with $2n$ (or $2n + 1$) digits: for example, $100 \ldots 001$, with $2n - 2$ (or $2n - 1$) 0s in the middle. If we change any of the digits in the right-hand half, then to obtain a palindrome we must change the corresponding digits in the left-hand half too. Thus the *next* palindromic year must change only *the middle two* digits if the number has $2n$ *digits* (or the one *middle* digit if the number has $2n + 1$ digits), and so will be $100 \ldots 0110 \ldots 001$ (or $100 \ldots 010 \ldots 001$) with a gap of $110 \ldots 000 = 10^n + 10^{n-1}$ (or $10 \ldots 000 = 10^n$). Hence there is no 'largest gap'.

B2 **How many years since AD 1 (up to 1991) used just two different digits?**

There are several ways of doing this. We choose a simple-minded, and hence rather long-winded, approach.

We count two-digit years first, then three-digit years, and finally four-digit years.

Two-digit years: There are 90 two-digit years between 10 and 99, of which 9 do *not* have two different digits: this gives $90 - 9 = 9 \times 9$ years with two different digits.

Three-digit years: There are 900 three-digit years between 100 and 999. In each 'hundred' (say from 100 to 199) there is *one number* which uses just one digit (111); so the number of years in each 'hundred' which uses two different digits is $100 - 1 - $ (*the number of years which use three different digits*).

Now count years which use *three different digits*. In each given 'hundred', the hundreds digit is fixed: there are then *nine* possibilities for the tens digit. And for *each* tens digits, there are *eight* possible units digits.

So in each 'hundred', there are 9×8 years which use three different digits; hence there are $100 - 1 - (9 \times 8) = 27$ years which use *two different digits*. So among all 900 three-digit years the number which use just two different digits is $9 \times (100 - 1 - (9 \times 8)) = 9 \times 27$.

Four-digit years: It seems sensible to follow the same pattern and to count *all* four-digit years beginning with a 1 which use just two different digits – that is, to count *all the way up to 1999* – and then to subtract the ones beyond 1991. (How many years between 1992 and 1999 use just two different digits?)

There are 1000 years between 1000 and 1999.

One of these uses a *one* repeated digit (1111).

How many years use *four different digits*? The thousand digit is fixed: there are then *nine* possibilities for the hundreds digit; and once this has been fixed, there are just *eight* possibilities for the tens digit; and once both these have been fixed, there are just *seven* possibilities for the units digit.

Hence there are $9 \times 8 \times 7$ years which use four different digits.

So the number of four-digit years up to 1999 which use two different digits is $1000 - 1 - 9 \times 8 \times 7 - $ (*the number of years which use just three different digits*). So if we manage to count how many four-digit years beginning with a 1 use just three different digits, we will be home and dry.

A four-digit year which uses *three* different digits has *one* digit repeated *twice*. If it is the '1' that is repeated, the number looks like:

$$1\ 1\ \bullet\ \bullet, \quad \text{or } 1\ \bullet\ 1\ \bullet, \quad \text{or } 1\ \bullet\ \bullet\ 1.$$

In each case there are *nine* possible ways of filling in the •; and once this digit has been chosen, there are then just *eight* choices for the ◆. There are therefore 9×8 years of each type, making $3 \times 9 \times 8$ altogether.

Now suppose the '1' is *not* repeated, but some other digit *is* repeated. Then the number looks like:

$$1\ \bullet\ \bullet\ \bullet, \quad \text{or } 1\ \bullet\ \bullet\ \bullet, \quad \text{or } 1\ \bullet\ \bullet\ \bullet.$$

In each case, there are *nine* possible ways of filling in the • ; and once this digit has been chosen, there are just *eight* choices for the ◆ . So again there are 9×8 years of each type, making $3 \times 9 \times 8$ altogether.

Hence the number of years from 1000 to 1999 which use *three different digits* is equal to $2 \times (3 \times 9 \times 8)$.

Therefore the number of years from 1000 to 1999 which use just two digits is

$$1000 - 1 - (9 \times 8 \times 7) - 2 \times (3 \times 9 \times 8) = \mathbf{63}.$$

We should not have counted 1999, so we must now subtract *one* to get **62**.

Thus the required number is $62 + 9 \times 27 + 9 \times 9 = \mathbf{386}$.

B3 **(a) Find the next perfect square after 9 that is equal to the sum of two different cubes.**
   (b) Can a perfect square ever be written as the sum of three squares?

(a) $9 = 3^2 = 1^3 + 2^3$. Write out a list of cubes:

$$1, 8, 27, 64, 125, 216, 343, 512, 729, 1000, 1331, 1728, \ldots$$

Now systematically check sums of pairs to see if you get a square:

$$1 + 27 = ?; \quad 1 + 64 = ?; \quad 1 + 125 = ?; \quad 1 + 216 = ?; \quad 1 + 343 = ?;$$
$$1 + 512 = ?; \quad 1 + 729 = ?; \ldots$$

$$8 + 27 = ?; \quad 8 + 64\ ?; \quad 8 + 125 = ?; \quad 8 + 216 = ?; \quad 8 + 343 = ?;$$
$$8 + 512 = ?; \quad 8 + 729 = ?; \ldots$$

$$27 + 64 = ?; \quad 27 + 125 = ?; \quad 27 + 216 = ?; \quad 27 + 343 = ?;$$
$$27 + 512 = ?; \quad 27 + 729 = ?; \ldots$$

$64 + 125 = ?;$ $64 + 216 = ?;$ $64 + 343 = ?;$ $64 + 512 = ?;$
$64 + 729 = ?;$ ...

$125 + 216 = ?;$ $125 + 343 = ?;$ $125 + 512 = ?;$ $125 + 729 = ?;$ ...

$216 + 343 = ?;$ $216 + 512 = ?;$ $216 + 729 = ?;$ ...

One of these works; which one is it?

There are all sorts of ways of making this search more efficient. For example, you should know that a square can only end in 0, 1, 4, 5, 6, or 9; this eliminates half of the above list without any work at all. $(64 + 512 = 576$ could be obtained very simply from $1 + 8 = 9$ by multiplying both sides by _____, which is both a square and a cube.)

(b) Write out a list of squares: 1, 4, 9, 16, 25, 36, 49, 64, 81, ...

Now combine them systematically *in threes*. There are lots of different solutions. $3^2 = 2^2 + 2^2 + 1^2$ is so obvious that you should realise straightaway that the interesting problem is to look for three *different* squares which add to a square. You should soon find the two easiest examples: $7^2 = 6^2 + 3^2 + 2^2$ and $9^2 = 8^2 + 4^2 + 1^2$, and perhaps $13^2 = 12^2 + 4^2 + 3^2$.

You might like to look for a way of generating all possible solutions of

$$n^2 = a^2 + b^2 + c^2$$

where n, a, b, c are positive integers. More precisely, given any two positive integers a, b, use $a^2 + b^2 = n^2 - c^2$ to find all possible pairs n, c.

(**Note:** If you thought the question asked for a square equal to the sum of three *cubes* you might have found $27^2 = 8^3 + 6^3 + 1^3$ $(= 9^3)$.)

B4 **For which values of N can an N-gon have successive sides always equal in length and at right angles?**

Let the sides be 1 unit long. If you draw a polygon with N sides starting from vertex A, you must return to A after N steps. Each time you go *north*, this has to be balanced by another move *south*; and each time you go *west*, this has to be balanced by another move *east*. Hence the total number of sides must be *even*.

Another way of seeing this is to observe that the angles of our polygon are either 90° or 270°. Suppose the polygon has x angles equal to 90° and y angles equal to 270°. Then $x + y$ is the total number of angles in the polygon, namely N; and $90x + 270y$ is the sum of all the angles in our polygon with N sides, which is always equal to $(N - 2) \times 180$; hence $x + 3y = 2N - 4$. Combining these two facts shows that $2y = N - 4$, so N must be even. If $N = 2n$, it follows that $y = n - 2$, $x = n + 2$.

A third approach is forget about *returning* to the start and ask how many *left* and *right* turns as we go round the polygon will leave us *facing in the same direction* as at the start. Each left turn can be 'cancelled' by a right turn, or by three more left turns, or by . . . In particular N must be even.

$N = \mathbf{4}$ can be realised as a square.

$N = \mathbf{6}$ requires $y = 1$, $x = 5$; if you start drawing the polygon from the 270° angle, it is clear that it cannot be completed.

$N = \mathbf{8}$ requires $y = 2$, $x = 6$. Starting from a 270° corner you get the same initial picture as in the previous case, and you are then forced to draw two squares joined at a corner, which is not a proper polygon.

Can $N = \mathbf{10}$? When you try to construct such a polygon, you will soon be convinced that it is impossible. However, you want a *mathematical* reason which will *prove* that it is impossible. The key here is to realise that it is not just $N = 10$ which is impossible! Look back at the way we showed that N had to be even. Concentrate on the sides which run in a *north–south* direction. Since sides going north have to be cancelled out by sides going south, the number of sides running north–south must *itself* be even – say $2m$. But the sides of the polygon alternate between north–south and east–west, so there must be exactly the same number of each type; hence $N = 2m + 2m$ has to be a multiple of 4.

$N = \mathbf{12}$ can be realised by a 'cross'.

$N = \mathbf{12 + 4k}$ is realised by extending this cross k steps southeast; the case $k = 2$ is illustrated here.

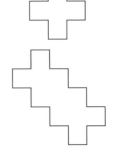

B5 Two walls, one of height *a* metres and the other of height *b* metres, are *d* metres apart. A ladder of length *l* metres has its feet hinged at a point between the two walls and can just reach the top of each. The two positions of the ladder are at right angles. How many different solutions are there for *a, b, d, l* if all four have to be positive integers less than 20?

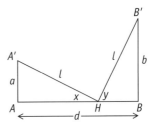

You are told that the two positions of the ladder are at right angles. Hence $x + y = 90°$. But then $\angle HA'A = y$ and $\angle HB'B = x$, so the two right-angled triangles are similar. Since the two hypotenuses are equal (of length *l*) it follows that $AH = b$, $HB = a$. Hence the positive whole numbers *a, b, l* satisfy $a^2 + b^2 = l^2$, and both $d = a + b$ and *l* must be less than 20. If $a \le b$ then there are just three possibilities:

$$(a, b, l, d) = (3, 4, 5, 7), (5, 12, 13, 17), (6, 8, 10, 14).$$

In general (allowing for the possibility $b > a$) we get six different solutions *a, b, l, d*.

B6 Eebs have honeycombs with square cells, all packed tightly together. An eeb grub starts in one cell. Each day it moves to a neighbouring cell, possibly revisiting a cell it occupied on a previous occasion.
   (a) Suppose it starts in a cell in the middle of the honeycomb. How many different cells would you have to look in to be sure of finding it on the *n*th day?
   (b) What if the grub starts in a corner cell? How many different cells would you have to look in to be sure of finding it on the *n*th day?

(a) We shall assume that 'neighbouring' cells have to have a whole wall in common. If the eeb starts in the middle of a very large chessboard, (on the grey square in the first diagram), then on the next day it can be in any one of the four neighbouring squares. On the third day it can be in any one of nine neighbouring squares. And so on. To see what is happening you have to turn the board through 45°. It should then be clear that the squares you have to look in on the *n*th day form a square *n* by *n* array.

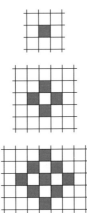

(b) If the eeb starts in a corner, everything is just as it was before except that you now have to look only in *one quadrant*.

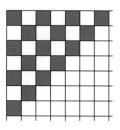

When n is odd, you have to look in
$1 + 3 + 5 + 7 + \ldots + n$ cells;

that is, in $\frac{(n+1)^2}{4}$ cells.

When n is even, you have to look in $2 + 4 + 6 + 8 + \ldots + n$ cells;

that is, in $\frac{n(n+2)}{4}$ cells.

1990: Section A

A1 1990 is ten times a prime number. What is the next number like this?

Not 10×201 (Why not?). How about 10×203?

To check whether a number like 203 is a prime number, you have to decide whether it can be factorised: $203 = a \times b$. So you have to look for possible factors. Factors come *in pairs* (a, b) – where $a \times b = 203$. If a is the smaller of the factors a, b, then $203 = a \times b \geq a^2$, so $\sqrt{203} \geq a$. Thus you only have to check possible factors up to the *square root* of 203, that is up to _____. Do this (no calculators!). The next two numbers to check are $10 \times$ _____ and $10 \times$ _____. Is 207 a prime number? Is 209 a prime number? Keep going.

A2 How many 6 cm by 8 cm tickets can be cut out of a 30 cm by 21 cm card?

The 30 cm by 21 cm card has area _____ cm^2, and each ticket has area _____ cm^2. $630 \div 48 =$ '13 and a bit'. This does not mean that the answer is 13, but it does show that it is impossible to get 14 tickets out of the given piece of card. Hence the answer must be 13 *or less*. Can you see how to get 10 tickets? Can you get 11? Can you get 12? *Can you get 13?*

A3 **How many prime numbers less than 10 000 have digits adding to 2?**

The smallest is 2. Any prime number bigger than 2 is odd, so if its digits add to 2 its first and last digits must both be 1s – with a string of 0s in between. Thus the next number like this is 11. Then _____. Finally _____. Which of these three numbers is not a prime?

A4 **The corners of a regular hexagon (in order) are _P, Q, R, S, T, U_. _PT_ and _SU_ cross at the point _V_. How big is the angle _TVS_?**

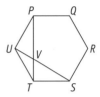

The hexagon is a *mathematical* hexagon – not a wooden one. And the question is a *mathematical* question, not one asked by a carpenter. So protractors are useless! We want to know the exact size of the perfect mathematical angle, so you must use perfect mathematical calculations.

Fill in the gaps in the following mathematical calculation, (and learn how to write out calculations like this for yourself).

The internal angle ∠*STU* in a regular hexagon has size _____°.

The triangle *STU* is i∗o∗∗e∗e∗   (because _____ = _____)

∴ ∠_____ = ∠_____   (base angles in an i∗o∗∗e∗e∗ triangle)

∴ ∠*TUS* = _____°.

Similarly triangle *TUP* is isosceles and ∠*UTP* = 30°.

∴ ∠*TVU* = _____°, so ∠*TVS* = _____°.

A5 **The digit 3 is written at the right of a certain two-digit number to make a three-digit number. The new number is 777 more than the original two-digit number. What was the original number?**

You have to find digits *a* and *b* so that '*ab*3' = '*ab*' + '777'. This tells you immediately that *b* = _____. Now put this digit in place of *b*, and work out that *a* = _____.

(**Note:** Remember that the question asked for the *original* number '*ab*', not the total '*ab*3'.)

A6 **An equilateral triangle and a regular hexagon have equal perimeters. Find the ratio of their areas.**

Simple properties of equilateral triangles and regular hexagons should be part of the stock-in-trade of all young mathematicians. The hexagon has *i* equal sides, while the triangle has ***ee. Thus, since the two shapes have equal perimeters, each side of the hexagon must have length exactly *a** the length of each side of the triangle. The 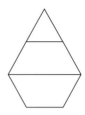 diagram on the right almost shouts out the other relevant fact, namely that the hexagon can be divided into *i* identical equilateral triangles while the big equilateral triangle can be cut into just *ou* such triangles. You should now be able to answer the question.

A7 **How far forward should the runner in the outside lane start in a one-lap race round a six-lane track (each lane 1 metre wide)?**

How far forward of *what*? The only sensible comparison is presumably with the runner in the i**i*e lane.

What shape is the track? You are not told. But the most obvious assumption is that it consists of two 'straights' with semi*i**u*a* ends. How much longer is the outside lane than the inside lane? A moment's thought should convince you which bits are different. (**Hint:** it isn't the straight bits!) So all you need to decide is the difference in the radii of the two circular bits. (**Hint:** for a six-lane track the difference in the radii of the inside semicircle and the outside semicircle is not six metres.)

A8 **The sun is 60° above the horizon. A vertical tree, 60 ft high, casts its shadow straight down a 30° slope. How long is the shadow?**

The sun, the tree, and the shadow *beg* you to draw a diagram. All that stuff about 30° and 60° means this is really a question about e*ui*a*e*a* triangles.

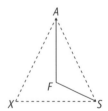

Let *FA* be the tree and *FS* the shadow down the slope.

Let *SX* be horizontal with *SX* = *SA*. Then △*SAX* is i*o**e*e*, with ∠*SAX* = ∠*SXA*. Moreover ∠*ASX* = ＿＿ (given), so ∠*SAX* = ＿＿ and triangle *ASX* is e*ui*a*e*a*. Extend *AF* to meet *SX* at *Y*; then ∠*AFS* = ＿＿ (since the tree *FA* is *e**i*a*), so ∠*FAS* = ＿＿. ∠*FSX* = ＿＿ (given), so ∠*FSA* = 60° − ∠*FSX* = ＿＿. Hence, ∠*SAX* = ＿＿ and △*FSA* is i*o**e*e*, so the shadow has length *FS* = *FA* = ＿＿.

A9 A new operation $\star$ for combining two numbers a and b is defined by $a \star b = \dfrac{(a+b)}{2}$. If $x\star (x \star 14) = x$, what is x?

The symbol $\star$ here does *not* mean 'multiply'. The question tells you that $a \star b = \dfrac{(a+b)}{2}$; that is, $a \star b$ is the *average* of the two numbers a and b. Once you realise this you should see the sense in treating the bracket $(x \star 14)$ as a single number: call it '?'. Then $x \star ? = x$ implies that we must have $? = \underline{\hspace{1cm}}$. Now solve $x \star 14 = x$.

A10 The sun rises at 04:43 in London. When does it rise in Cardiff (3° W)?

Draw a diagram (of a circle of latitude, centre O)! In L (= London) the sun is just rising (in the east). You want to know when it will rise at C (= Cardiff). You are told that the arc LC subtends an angle at the centre O equal to $\underline{\hspace{1cm}}$.

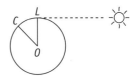

So the Earth will rotate from C to L in $\frac{3}{360}$ of the time it takes the Earth to turn round exactly once. Well, how long does it take for the Earth to go round once? So how long does it take for radius OC to rotate to the vertical position in the diagram?

1990: Section B

B1 **In how many different ways can one trace out MATHS?**

Do not try to count all the possibilities by tracing
them with your pen! You need a mathematical
idea to break the problem into manageable bits.
One idea is to realise that the figure is made up
of four 'quarters', like the bit shown here
(though the quarters overlap slightly, so some
care is needed). However, there are still too many paths to count all at once –
criss-crossing their way from the *M* to one of the *S*s.

```
S
H  S
T  H  S
A  T  H  S
M  A  T  H  S
```

Idea: Count the words which end at each *S* *separately*.

There is clearly just one way of starting at the central *M* and ending at the
bottom *S*. How many ways are there of finishing up at *S* on the end of the
second row from the bottom? (This is not too hard, but you still have to be
careful.) And how many ways are there of ending at the middle *S*? If you keep
your wits about you, you should recognise the numbers you are getting, and
may discover another mathematical idea which removes all possibility of
making a mistake.

B2 **'y pounds and x pence' minus one pound is twice 'x pounds and y pence'.**
Find x and y.

Use the information given to set up an equation: y pounds and x pence is equal
to _____ pence; after spending £1, that leaves _____ pence; you are told that
this is twice as much as originally asked for. This can be written as an
equation linking x, y. Unfortunately this is not the kind of equation you may
be used to, for there are *two* unknowns, but only *one* equation. However, since
this is a question about money, you know that the numbers x and y have to be
**o*e numbers. If you write the equation in the form $199x = 98y - 100$, then
the RHS is the difference of two e*e* numbers, so the LHS (and hence x)
must be e*e*. If you play around with the equation, you should be able to
show that $2y - x$ has to be a multiple of 100. Since

> y pounds and x pence is slightly more than double x pounds and y pence,
> y must be slightly more than twice x.

The simplest possible case is $2y - x = 100$. Thus x must be a bit less than
_____. This should give you one solution. Are there any other possible
solutions? (The fact that the question is about *money* comes in at this point!)

B3 **Which numbers cannot be made up exactly using a combination of 5s, 9s, and 12s?**

Trial and error can be a good way of getting started: but you must *be systematic*. For example, it is easy to see that ≤4 is impossible; 5 is OK; 6–8 are impossible; 9 is OK; 10 is OK; 11 is impossible; 12 is OK; and so on. What you discover should suggest that *from some point on*, every number can be obtained. But how can you be sure that *all* numbers in the millions or beyond can be made? You need a mathematical *idea*. Suppose you notice that

45 = five ___ s,   46 = three ___ s and two ___s,

47 = seven ___ s and a___,   48 = four ___s,

49 = two ___s and five ___s.

How can you be absolutely sure that 50 can be obtained *without working it out*? (50 = _____ + **5**) And how can you be absolutely sure that 51 can be obtained *without working it out*? (51 = _____ + **5**) And what about 52? 53? 54? 55? ... ? Now work backwards from 44, 43, ... ?

B4 **A cylindrical barrel of diameter 1 metre lies on its side right up against a wall. How big a ball will fit in the gap between the barrel and the wall?**

Draw a clear diagram and then look at it carefully. The diameter of the ball is definitely not $OP - OA = AP$ (Why not?). The diameter is A___.

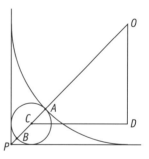

Method 1: One beautiful, but simple, approach is to notice that the gap between the ball and the corner is *similar* to the gap between the barrel and the corner. Use this idea to complete the following solution. Suppose the ball has radius r metres. Then $OP = 1 + 2r + BP$. Now OP is the *y*o*e*u*e of an isosceles right-angled triangle, with sides of length 1, so $OP = $ _____. Hence $\sqrt{2} = 1 + 2r + BP$. Similarly $CP = \sqrt{2}.r = r + BP$. Subtracting these equations gives $\sqrt{2}(1 - r) = 1 + r$, so $r = $ _____.

Method 2: Another approach highlights a useful general principle: in geometry, always mark in the centres of all circles. Let O be the centre of the barrel and C the centre of the ball. If the radius of the ball is r, then $OC = 1 + r$, and $CD = OD = 1 - r$. Hence Pythagoras' theorem gives $1 + r = \sqrt{2}(1 - r)$, so $r = $ _____.

107

B5 (a) $3^2 = 9$ is very nearly the average of two other squares. Find them.
  (b) Find three squares where one is exactly the average of the other two.
  (c) Show that there are infinitely many such triples.

(a) If $3^2 = 9$ is very nearly the *average* of two other squares, they must have sum roughly equal to 2×9. Hence the two squares must be _____ and _____ (with average equal to $8\frac{1}{2}$).

(b) You now have to find three squares where the middle one is *exactly* the average of the other two. You should soon come up with 1, 25, 49 (since $1 + 49 = 50$), though it may take a while before you find your second triple.

Once you find $(\text{\_\_\_\_\_})^2 + (\text{\_\_\_\_\_})^2 = 2 \times 5^2$ and $(\text{\_\_\_\_\_})^2 + (\text{\_\_\_\_\_})^2 = 2 \times 10^2$ all sorts of bells should start ringing. How do these two solutions immediately lead to *infinitely* many triples?

B6 (a) How many winning lines in 4 by 4 noughts and crosses? *n* by *n*?
  (b) How many winning lines in *n* by *n* by *n* noughts and crosses?

(a) This is an excellent example of real mathematics.

To deal with an *n* by *n* noughts and crosses we are going to need a little a∗∗e∗∗a. Algebra is a way of capturing *complete generality of method by using symbols to represent the general case.*

In this problem, the general case is an *n* by *n* game of noughts and crosses. We *gain insight* into the *general* case by studying particular cases *in the right way*. So we must try to count the winning lines on a 3 by 3 and 4 by 4 board in a way which will help us count winning lines on an *n* by *n* board. To see what happens on an *n* by *n* board, try to express what happens on a 3 by 3 board in *general terms*. (This is quite different from 'pattern spotting'. You should not be trying to *guess*. Instead, look carefully and try to understand exactly what is going on.)

	3 by 3 board	4 by 4 board	*n* by *n* board
Number of *horizontal* winning lines	= (3 rows) × (1 in each row)	= (4 rows) × (__ in each row)	= n × _____
Number of *vertical* winning lines	= (3 cols) × (1 in each col.)	= (4 cols) × (__ in each col.)	= n × _____
Number of *sloping* winning lines	= (2 diags) × (1 in each diag.)	= 2 × __ + 4 × __	= _____? _____

108

This leaves you in no doubt that the only awkward bit is counting the number of ways of getting 'three-in-a-line' *diagonally*. To get this right, you must be very careful (or discover some clever mathematical idea which makes counting them very easy). Once you have managed to count the diagonal winning lines, you have to add the three subtotals to get the total. When you come to do this, remember that your *answers should always be given in simple form*. It is no good just adding the three bits and leaving it at that. *You must simplify your answer* into the most compact, useful form you can find. (The answer is in fact 8 times a triangular number!)

(b) Part (b) is similar (though you now have to count horizontal front to back as well as horizontal left to right; and there are several different kinds of diagonals). Because of these extra complications you are unlikely to get away with just being careful. When things get tough, don't give up. Look for an idea! (In particular, look for an idea which makes a 4 by 4 by 4 game easy once you can do a 3 by 3 by 3 game!)

	Horizontal front–back	Horizontal left–right	Vertical top–down	'Slice' diagonals	Body diagonals
Number of winning lines on $3 \times 3 \times 3$	(9 rows)× (1 per row)	(9 rows)× (1 per row)	_____ × _____	(3 × 3 slices)× (2 per slice)	_____ _____
Number of winning lines on $4 \times 4 \times 4$	(____ rows)× (__ per row)	(____ rows)× (__ per row)	_____ × _____	_____ slices × (__ per slice)	_____ _____

You should try to count the winning lines on an *n* by *n* by *n* board in a similar way.

- You will need to use your answer to part (a) to count the number of diagonals which occur in the 3*n* possible *n* by *n* 'slices'.
- You will need to be careful when counting the winning lines which do not lie in one of these slices (these are what we have called 'body diagonals').
- And when you add everything up at the end, you must simplify your answer as much as possible.

It is often true in mathematics that one struggles to solve a problem only to find an answer which suggests there must have been a much easier way!

1989

1 Find the smallest multiple of 9 with no odd digits.

You could just write out all multiples of 9 until you find one with no odd digits. This approach is not satisfactory and tends to lead to rather basic errors. A more mathematical approach is to notice that

(i)   9 is odd, so if all digits are to be even, you only need worry about *even* multiples of 9 – that is, *multiples* of 18;

(ii) every multiple of 9 up to 100 has either an odd tens or an odd units digit;

(iii) every multiple of 9 from 100 to 199 has an odd hundreds digit.

Thus you need only worry about multiples of 18 above 200. Since each multiple of 9 has digits adding to a multiple of 9 (*not* to 9 itself as many students seem to believe), multiples of 9 in the 200s must have digits adding to 9 or to 18. If all three digits are to be even, then the digits must add to 18 (since a digit sum of 9 would require at least one odd digit). For numbers in the 200s the hundreds digit is 2, so the tens and units digits must add to _____. Thus the first number we really have to try is _____.

2 Explain how to cut both regions exactly in half with one cut.

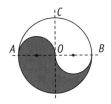

Where the two internal semicircles meet (at the centre O of the large circle), they are both vertical. The other ends A, B of the two semicircles lie at opposite ends of the horizontal diameter AOB of the big circle. This suggests a natural origin O, y-axis OC, and x-axis AOB. Let r be the radius of the large circle. Then the area of the top left quadrant AOC is _____ and the area of the shaded semicircle with diameter AO is _____. Hence the left-hand semicircle divides the top left quadrant AOC exactly in *a*. The other semicircle does the same to the bottom right quadrant. So all you have to do is to divide the top right quadrant (white) and the bottom left quadrant (shaded) in half with a single straight cut through O. How to cut should now be clear.

3 How could you multiply 7 628 954 301 by 125 in your head?

Surprisingly few candidates recognised the basic fact that $125 = 1000 \div 8$. So all we have to do is to put three 0s on the end of the ten-digit number, and then divide by 8. Check that this leads to a way of 'multiplying 7 628 954 301 by 125' that one really could 'do in one's head' (provided the ten-digit number was written down).

4 Joining each vertex in the big regular hexagon to the next vertex but one produces a smaller hexagon inside. Prove that the smaller hexagon is regular. Find its edge length in terms of the edge length of the big hexagon.

In this instance a *proof* should combine *in a very precise way*

(i)   what you are *told* about the big hexagon – namely that it is *regular*, and

(ii) general geometrical *results* (such as that the base angles of an isosceles triangle are always equal).

You must then start out from *what you know is true*, and proceed *one step at a time* until you manage to *deduce the result you want to prove*.

Fill in the missing details in the following skeleton proof.

$AB = BC$ (since *ABCDEF* is $*e*u*a*$)

$\therefore \angle BAC = \angle BCA$ (since $\triangle ABC$ is $i*o**e*e*$)

$\qquad = \frac{1}{2}(180° - \angle ABC) = \underline{\qquad}.$

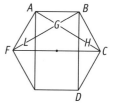

Similarly, $\triangle FAB$ is isosceles and $\angle ABF = 30°$

$\therefore \angle LGH = \angle AGB$ (vertically opposite angles)

$\qquad = 180° - \angle GAB - \angle GBA = 120°$

Hence the angle at the vertex G in the inside hexagon has size 120°. The same reasoning shows that each angle of the inside hexagon has size 120°.

A hexagon with all six angles equal to 120° need not be regular (Why?). Thus we must prove that any two adjacent sides of the inside hexagon – such as *LG* and *GH* – have the same length. For this we use the ASA congruence criterion to prove that $\triangle GLA$ and $\triangle GHB$ are congruent.

$\angle GBH = \angle ABC - \angle ABG - \angle DBC = 120° - 30° - 30° = \underline{\qquad}.$

Similarly $\angle LAG = 60°$, so (i) $\angle LAG = \angle GBH$

Moreover, $\triangle GAB$ is isosceles (since $\angle BAC = \angle ABF = 30°$), so (ii) $GA = GB$.

Finally (iii) $\angle LGA = \angle HGB$ (*e**i*a**y o**o*i*e angles).

Conditions (i), (ii) and (iii) imply that $\triangle GLA$ and $\triangle GHB$ are congruent (ASA).

Hence $LG = HG$ as required.

It remains to calculate the length GH in terms of AB.

Now $GA = GB$, and $HB = HC$ (since $\triangle GAB$ and $\triangle HBC$ are both i*o**e*e*). Moreover, $\angle GBH =$ _____, $\angle BHG = 180° - \angle BGA =$ _____, and $\angle BGH =$ _____, so $\triangle GBH$ is e*ui*a*e*a*.

Therefore $GB = GB = HB$; hence $AG = GH = HC$, and $AC = 3.GH$.

$\triangle GAB$ and $\triangle GCF$ are *i*i*a* (since $\angle AGB = \angle CGF$ (vertically opposite angles), $\angle GAB = \angle GCF =$ _____, and $\angle GBA = \angle GFC =$ _____). Hence

$$AB : CF = GA : GC = GA : (GH + HC) = 1 : 2; \text{ so } CF = 2.AB.$$

Finally, $\angle FAC = \angle FAB - \angle GAB = 120° - 30° =$ _____. Thus we may use *y**a*o*a* theorem on $\triangle FAC$ to calculate GH.

$$(2.AB)^2 = FC^2 = FA^2 + AC^2 = AB^2 + (3.GH)^2$$
$$\therefore GH = \frac{1}{\sqrt{3}}. AB$$

5 Find two perfect squares that differ by 105. How many different solutions are there?

Finding one pair of squares that differ by exactly 105 should not be too hard (there are two such squares less than $12^2 = 144$). But that is only a beginning. The interesting bit is to *find all possible pairs*.

One approach is to observe that the difference between successive squares 1, 4, 9, 16, 25, . . . is always an odd number, and that the gap increases as the squares increase. The gap between 4^2 and 5^2 is exactly $2 \times 4 + 1$. How far must you go before the gap between successive squares is *too big*?

The gap between N^2 and $(N + 1)^2$ is $2N + 1$, and $2N + 1 = 105$ when $N =$ _____.

Thus you do not need to worry about squares bigger than 53^2, so checking all possible pairs of squares is a finite task. If you try this approach you will probably make mistakes without noticing. A more mathematical approach is to write the squares as a^2 and b^2, and to look for (positive) whole numbers a, b satisfying the equation

$$a^2 - b^2 = 105.$$

As soon as you see the difference of two squares on the left-hand side you should feel an irresistable urge to *a**o*i*e it. The two algebraic factors you then have on the left-hand side must correspond to some factorisation of the right-hand side.

Factorise 105 as a product of three prime factors.

Hence find the four different factorisations of 105:

$$105 = 105 \times \text{\_\_\_\_}; \quad 105 = \text{\_\_\_\_} \times \text{\_\_\_\_};$$

$$105 = \text{\_\_\_\_} \times \text{\_\_\_\_}; \quad 105 = \text{\_\_\_\_} \times \text{\_\_\_\_}.$$

Since a and b are whole numbers, with a bigger than b, $a + b$ and $a - b$ must be whole numbers with $a + b$ bigger than $a - b$. Each of the four factorisations above correspond to a pair of simultaneous equations

$$a + b = \text{\_\_\_\_}, \quad a - b = \text{\_\_\_\_},$$

which you can solve to find the four possible pairs a, b.

6 **A right-angled triangle has legs of length a and b. A circle of radius r touches the two legs and has its centre on the hypotenuse. Show that**

$$\frac{1}{a} + \frac{1}{b} = \frac{1}{r}.$$

Of those who drew the correct diagram, very few drew in the *two really important lines OX* and *OY* (both of length r), which would have shown that this question is really about *similar right-angled triangles*.

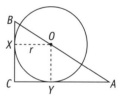

Method 1:

$$\frac{OY}{BC} = \frac{OA}{BA} \quad \text{(since triangles } OYA \text{ and } BCA \text{ are similar),}$$

$$\frac{OX}{AC} = \frac{OB}{AB} \quad \text{(since triangles } OXB \text{ and } ACB \text{ are similar),}$$

$$\therefore 1 = \frac{OA+OB}{AB} = \frac{OY}{BC} + \frac{OX}{AC} = \frac{r}{a} + \frac{r}{b};$$

$$\therefore \frac{1}{r} = \frac{1}{a} + \frac{1}{b}.$$

Method 2: Three or four candidates discovered a rather clever solution based on areas. The two important lines of length r which you have drawn cut the original triangle into three bits: two triangles and one square. If you add up the areas of the three bits, you must get the area $\frac{(ab)}{2}$ of the original triangle. This gives you an equation. Write down this equation and use it to show that $\frac{1}{a} + \frac{1}{b} = \frac{1}{r}$.

7 Find all pairs (x, y) whose sum, product, and quotient are all equal.

You clearly have to solve the equations $x + y = x.y = \frac{x}{y}$. No one said that the solutions have to be whole numbers, or even positive numbers. You may be tempted to suggest $x = 0$, $y = 0$ as one solution. But what does $\frac{0}{0}$ mean? In mathematics, dividing by 0 is forbidden – it makes no sense! (Can you see why not?) Thus y cannot be 0. Could $x = 0$?

Thus you may assume that $x \neq 0$. You may then be tempted to think that $x.y = \frac{x}{y}$ means that y has to be 1. If so, think again! The equation $xy = \frac{x}{y}$ can be rewritten as $xy^2 = x$, so $y^2 = $ _____ (since $x \neq 0$). Hence $y = + 1$, or $y = $ _____.

If $y = + 1$, the equation $x + y = x.y$ becomes $x + 1 = x$, which has no solutions.

If $y = - 1$, the equation $x + y = x.y$ becomes $x - 1 = - x$, so $x = $ _____.

8 An equilateral triangle with sides of length 3 is cut into nine equilateral triangles of side length 1. Place the numbers 1 to 9 in the nine small triangles so that the sum of the numbers inside any equilateral triangle with side length 2 is the same. What are the smallest and largest possible values of this sum?

The triangle of side length 3 contains just *three* triangles of side length 2. These triangles of side length 2 overlap in the shaded triangles. If the sum of the numbers in each triangle of side length 2 is S, then adding the three totals for the triangles of side length 2 gives _____ + _____ + _____ = _____.

Now the three triangles with side length 2 use up all the small triangles at least once, and the shaded triangles exactly **i**e. Thus $3S$ must be equal to the sum of the numbers in all the small triangles with each shaded triangle counted **i**e. But the numbers in the small triangles are just the numbers 1–9.

You can now write down an equation linking S and the sum of the numbers in the three shaded triangles. To make S as small as possible, you must make the entries in the three shaded triangles as **a** as possible. And to make S as large as possible, you must make the entries in the three shaded triangles as *a**e as possible.

9 If $a^2 + b^2 + c^2 = ab + bc + ca$, must a, b, c all be equal?

You are given three positive real numbers a, b, c which satisfy

$$a^2 + b^2 + c^2 = ab + bc + ca.$$

You then have to decide whether this equation can *only* be true if $a = b = c$.

Watch your logic! You are *definitely* not meant just to check that

- when $a = b = c$, the LHS $= 3a^2$ and the RHS $= 3a^2$, so $a^2 + b^2 c^2 = ab + bc + ca$.

You have to *prove* the precise opposite of this, namely that

- when $a^2 + b^2 + c^2 = ab + bc + ca$, the only possibility is $a = b = c$.

This is quite different: you have to *start* with the given equation, and then *prove* that $a = b = c$ – *not* the other way round.

The proof depends on the simple, but important, algebraic fact that

$$(\star) \quad (a - b)^2 = a^2 - 2ab + b^2.$$

Moreover, since $(a - b)^2$ is a *square*, its value cannot be ∗e∗a∗i∗e. *Use this fact to fill in the gaps in the following skeleton proof.*

Suppose that a, b, c satisfy the equation

$$a^2 + b^2 + c^2 = ab + bc + ca;$$

$$\therefore 2(a^2 + b^2 + c^2) = 2(\underline{} + \underline{} + \underline{}).$$

Taking all terms to the LHS and rearranging them cleverly to make use of $(\star)$,

$$\therefore a^2 - 2ab + b^2 + \underline{} + \underline{} = 0;$$

$$\text{that is, } (\underline{})^2 + (\underline{})^2 + (\underline{})^2 = 0.$$

But the squares cannot possibly be ∗e∗a∗i∗e. So the only way they can cancel out to give zero is if each of the three terms on the left-hand side is equal to ∗e∗o.

$$\therefore (\underline{}) = 0, (\underline{}) = 0, \text{ and } (\underline{}) = 0;$$

$$\therefore a = b = c.$$

10 Pythagoras' theorem for the right-angled triangle *ABC* is often illustrated by a diagram like the one shown here (without the dotted lines). Putting in the three dotted lines shows that the whole figure can be enclosed in a hexagon. Find the area of this hexagon in terms of the edge lengths *a*, *b*, *c* of the original triangle.

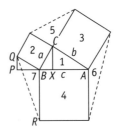

If we divide the hexagon into seven separate regions as shown, then you should be able to write down simple formulae for the following five areas:

$$\text{area 1} = \underline{\hspace{2em}}; \quad \text{area 2} = \underline{\hspace{2em}}; \quad \text{area 3} = \underline{\hspace{2em}};$$

$$\text{area 4} = \underline{\hspace{2em}}; \quad \text{area 5} = \underline{\hspace{2em}}.$$

Thus the real challenge is to work out *area 6 and area 7* in terms of *a*, *b*, *c*. (Make sure you can see why the answer is *not* 'area 6 = $\frac{bc}{2}$, area 7 = $\frac{ca}{2}$'.)

Mathematics is full of surprises. It turns out that area 5, area 6, and area 7 are related in a rather unexpected way. See if you can discover this for yourself before reading on.

There are several formulae for the area of a triangle, but they all boil down to '$\frac{1}{2}$ base × height'. So to find area 7, for example, you must *choose a base*. If you take the base of area 7 as the side *BR* of length *c*, then the height of the triangle is the perpendicular height *BP*. Now prove that triangles *BPQ* and *BCX* are *congruent*. Hence show that triangles *ABC* and *BQR* have equal area. You should now be in a position to finish off the solution on your own.

11 (a) **Find a square (other than 5^2, 10^2, 15^2, . . .) which is the sum of two squares.**

  (b) **Find a cube (other than 6^3, 12^3, 18^3, . . .) which is the sum of three cubes.**

Intelligent searching is an important part of mathematics.

(a) A list of squares is likely to be useful, so jot them down (the squares up to 225 should be engraved on your heart, so you should not have to do much 'calculating' to produce this list):

$$1^2 = \underline{\hspace{2em}}, \quad 2^2 = \underline{\hspace{2em}}, \quad 3^2 = \underline{\hspace{2em}}, \quad 4^2 = \underline{\hspace{2em}},$$

$$5^2 = \underline{\hspace{2em}}, \quad 6^2 = \underline{\hspace{2em}}, \quad 7^2 = \underline{\hspace{2em}}, \quad \ldots$$

Now check each one in turn:

$6^2 = ? + ?$ (the biggest possible square on the RHS must be $\leq 5^2$)

$7^2 = ? + ?$ (the biggest possible square on the RHS must be $\leq$ _____)

$8^2 = ? + ?$ (the biggest possible square on the RHS must be $\leq$ _____)

etc, until you find a square which is equal to the sum of two other squares.

(b) A list of cubes is likely to be useful, so jot them down (keep going up to 13^3 at least):

$$1^3 = \text{\_\_\_\_\_}, \quad 2^3 = \text{\_\_\_\_\_}, \quad 3^3 = \text{\_\_\_\_\_}, \quad 4^3 = \text{\_\_\_\_\_},$$

$$5^3 = \text{\_\_\_\_\_}, \quad 6^3 = \text{\_\_\_\_\_}, \quad 7^3 = \text{\_\_\_\_\_}, \quad \ldots$$

Now check each one in turn.

12 **Two straight cuts, one through each of two vertices of a triangle, divide the triangle into three smaller triangles and one quadrilateral.**
(a) Is it possible for the areas of all four parts to be equal?
(b) More generally, if three of the parts have area p while the fourth has area q, what are the possible values of $\frac{p}{q}$?

(a) *Suppose* all four regions could have the same area.

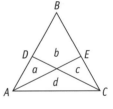

Then $a + b = c + d$, so triangles ABE and _____ must then have the same area. One of these triangles has base BE, the other has base CE, and they both have the same *ei***. Hence $BE = CE$, so E must be the *i**oi** of BC.

Similarly D must be the midpoint of AB. But then $AD = DB$, which forces $a < b$ (Why?).

(b) This part requires some ingenuity. Try to fill in the gaps for yourself.

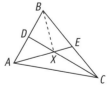

(i) Suppose first that area $(BDXE) = b = q$. Show that $DX = XC$, $AX = XE$, and that triangles ADX and ECX must then be congruent. Deduce that AD and CE would then have to be parallel.

(ii) Suppose next that area $(CEX) = c = q$, and let $\frac{p}{q} = x$.

Step 1: Show that $\frac{AX}{XE} = x$.

Step 2: Let p' be the area of triangle DBX. Show $\frac{(p+p')}{(p-p')} = x$ (use $\triangle ABX$ and $\triangle BEX$).

Step 3: Show $DX = XC$.

Step 4: Show $p - p' + \left(\frac{p}{x}\right) = p'$ (use $\triangle DXB$ and $\triangle CXB$), then find $\frac{p}{q} = x$ from Step 2.

(iii) Finally suppose area $(ACX) = d = q$. $\triangle BEX$ is part of region b so has area yp with $y < 1$.

Step 1: Show that $\frac{(1+y)}{(1-y)} = \frac{AX}{XE} = \frac{q}{p}$, and also that $y = \frac{2p}{(p+q)}$.

Step 2: Substitute for y in the first equation and solve for $\frac{p}{q}$.

13 Mr and Mrs A invite some other married couples to dinner. As they all meet, some pairs shake hands. Married couples do not shake hands with one another. Over coffee, while Mr A is washing up, the rest discover that they all shook hands a different number of times.
   (a) Suppose there were four couples altogether (including Mr and Mrs A). Can you say how many hands Mr A must have shaken?
   (b) What if there were five couples altogether? Can you say how many hands Mr A must have shaken?

(a) This is not nearly as hard as you might think. Read the question carefully. No one shakes hands more than _____ times. When Mr A is washing up, the seven others discover that they each shook hands a different number of times. So these seven different numbers *have to be*

_____, _____, _____, _____, _____, _____, _____.

Think hard about the person (say B) who shook hands *the most*. B must have shaken hands with everybody except their partner (B'). This means that all these other people (excluding B') must have shaken hands at least _____. In particular, this implies that B cannot be Mrs A (why not?). So how many hands did B' shake? Now think hard about the person (say C) who shook hands five times. Can you say how many hands their partner (C') must have shaken? Carry on like this.

(b) The idea here is exactly the same as for part (a).

Answers to Section A problems

The Junior Olympiad papers 1989–95

1995

A1 123   **A2** 60°   **A3** $\frac{4}{5}$

A4 £1.43   **A5** 400 cm^2 **A6** $\frac{26}{65}$

A7 108 cm^2 **A8** 30   **A9** 120

A10 14 : 11

1994

A1 105°   **A2** 14   **A3** $\frac{13}{15}$

A4 $\frac{17}{36}$ **A5** 75°   **A6** 32

A7 3   **A8** 1998   **A9** 540°

A10 39

1993

A1 8   **A2** 40 square units   **A3** $\frac{10}{9}$

A4 $5\frac{1}{2}$m   **A5** 6 and 10   **A6** $\frac{5}{6}$

A7 $(25a, 25b)$ **A8** $\frac{7\sqrt{3}}{2}$ **A9** The easiest answers are 1.40 and 10.20.

A10 41

1992

A1 1001   **A2** $\frac{3}{4}$ cm   **A3** 16

A4 6   **A5** $\frac{5}{11}$ **A6** $(4 + \pi)$ metres

A7 $(1 - \frac{\pi}{4})$ square metres   **A8** 5   **A9** 1700 km/h

A10 185

1991

A1 181   **A2** 32 hours   **A3** 30°

A4 45   **A5** $(6\sqrt{3})$ cm^2 **A6** 120

A7 $\sqrt{3} : 2$ **A8** b **A9** $(5\sqrt{2})$ cm

A10 7

1990

A1 2110   **A2** 12   **A3** 3

A4 60°   **A5** 86   **A6** $2 : 3$

A7 (10π) metres   **A8** 60 ft   **A9** 14

A10 4:55am

Additional Section A problems

1 $\frac{18}{11}$ and $\frac{40}{11}$

2 75 gallons

3 6

4 $\frac{2}{\pi}$

5 $\frac{1}{2}$

6 4 minutes

7 $\sqrt{2}$

8 2

9 111 111 111

10 $\frac{1}{5}$

11 23 456 789

12 $2r$

13 15

14 1 hour

15 27

16 9

17 $2\pi r$

18 −10

19 1 097 393 685

20 12

21 29 miles

22 333 333 332 666 666 667

23 1 cm

24 999 009 cm = 9.990 09 km

25 50°

26 22

27 πD

28 $\frac{y^3}{x^2}$

29 $\sqrt{1+4\pi^2}$

30 24

31 $\sqrt{3} - \left(\frac{\pi}{2}\right)$

32 $1 + \left(\frac{3\sqrt{3}}{4}\right)$

33 25

34 $\frac{1}{4}$

35 $\frac{5}{2}$

36 Impossible

37 $\frac{1}{3}$

38 48 (all except the eight equilateral triangles)

39 72 341

40 $\left(\frac{16\pi}{3}\right) - 4\sqrt{3}$

Additional resources

I hope the book list at the end of this section will be of interest to all readers – young and old. However, the comments preceding the book list are aimed primarily at teachers (though others may still find them of interest).

Trying to find suitable 'enrichment' material for more able youngsters can be frustrating. Though the need is widespread, there are few ready-made resources. So the first thing to stress is that there is no magic package of materials out there just waiting to be discovered. Each of us has to build up a (small) repertoire of books and activities that we know well, which we like, and which we can use flexibly.

What sort of materials are most effective will depend to some extent on the interests and enthusiasms of the individual teacher who is using them. However, I would like to risk one generalisation which has proved its validity time and again in my own work.

Adolescents, no matter how keen and talented they may be, are not very good at reading mathematical texts systematically. They may love science fiction; and they may occasionally dip into some 'higher mathematics' books – lying neglected and unread on the top shelves of the school library. However, this is unlikely to be the main way in which their interest in, and love of, mathematics will be nurtured. One reason is that such books are written by adults for an adult audience. But there is a deeper reason:

> such books encourage *passivity*,
> whereas the adolescent learns and grows by being *active*.

Moreover

> a text is, by its very nature, *systematic*,
> whereas adolescents often absorb ideas *unsystematically*.

Two things follow from this. The first is that the main source of adolescent mathematical enrichment is through *puzzles*, *problems* and *activities*. A starting list of such resources which I have found especially useful is given below. The list is deliberately *short*, and is restricted to books which should be generally available – though not all of them are still in print. Teachers will want to add to this list on the basis of their own experience (and will no doubt delete some items which they find less appealing). However, I would stress that, since we are concerned with *mathematical* enrichment, most ordinary 'puzzle books' are of limited value. When choosing resources, one needs a clear conception of how the activities will contribute to pupils' *mathematical* development. This contribution is not always apparent on the surface. For example, it may be tempting to dismiss origami as mere model making; yet many highly talented young mathematicians clearly revel in visualising and memorising more and more complicated sequences of folds.

The second thing is that if you do ply such youngsters with systematic texts, let them be texts that encourage *mathematical* activity; that is, texts with lots of exercises and problems designed for, and challenging to, interested and intelligent beginners. Fortunately, in school storerooms and second-hand bookshops, there are plenty of excellent old textbooks for teachers to choose from (for example, the many texts written by Snell and Morgan, by Durell, by Durell and Robson, by Godfrey and Siddons, by Hall and Knight, by Barnard and Child, etc.), which cover important and challenging material not currently taught in most of our schools, and which contain many well-designed exercises and problems. However, you do need to choose carefully. All books make assumptions about what the reader knows; given the time-warp, some of these assumptions may no longer be satisfied by even your best pupils. There is nothing wrong with that as long as the mismatch is not too great, and as long as you are aware of the extent of the problem *in advance*.

Booklist

Edwin A Abbott *Flatland: a romance in many dimensions*, Dover 1992
(also Blackwell 1962)

Brian Bolt *The amazing mathematical amusement arcade*,
Cambridge 1984
Mathematical funfair, Cambridge 1989
(numerous other titles by the same author)

Maxey Brooke *Tricks, games and puzzles with matches*, Dover 1973

M Cundy and A P Rollett *Mathematical models*, Oxford University Press
1961, now published by Tarquin, Diss, 1985

Joost Elfers *Tangram*, Penguin 1976

Eric Emmet *The Puffin book of brainteasers*, Puffin 1976

A Gardiner *Mathematical puzzling*, Oxford University Press 1987 (reprinted by UK Mathematics Foundation 1996)
Discovering mathematics, Oxford University Press 1987
The mathematical olympiad handbook, Oxford University Press 1997

Tony Gardiner *Mathematical challenge*, Cambridge University Press 1996

Martin Gardner *Mathematical puzzles of Sam Loyd*, Dover
Mathematical puzzles and diversions, Pelican 1965
More mathematical puzzles and diversions, Pelican 1966
Further mathematical puzzles and diversions, Pelican 1977
Mathematical carnival, Pelican 1978
Mathematical circus, Pelican 1981
Riddles of the sphinx, Mathematical Association of America 1987
(numerous other titles by the same author)

Boris Kordemsky *The Moscow puzzles*, Pelican 1975

Ya I Perelman *Algebra can be fun*, Mir Publishers 1979

SMP 11–16 *New stretchers*, Cambridge University Press 1991

Raymond Smullyan *What is the name of this book?*, Pelican 1981
The lady and the tiger, Penguin 1984
(numerous other titles by the same author)

Hugo Steinhaus *Mathematical snapshots*, Oxford University Press 1969
One hundred problems of elementary mathematics, Dover 1979

Ian Stewart *Game, set and math*, Penguin 1989
(numerous other titles by the same author)

Charles W Trigg *Mathematical quickies*, Dover 1967

Ravi Vakil *A mathematical mosaic*, Brendan Kelly Publishing Inc. 1996

David Wells *Can you solve these 1*, Tarquin 1982
Can you solve these 2, Tarquin 1984
Can you solve these 3, Tarquin 1986
Penguin dictionary of curious and interesting numbers, Penguin 1986
Penguin dictionary of curious and interesting geometry, Penguin 1991
Penguin book of curious and interesting puzzles, Penguin 1992
You are a mathematician, Penguin 1995

Magnus J Wenninger *Polyhedron models*, Cambridge University Press 1971

At some stage pupils may want to read books of general interest, or more serious 'texts' on specific mathematical topics. The following two lists may then provide some useful starters.

General interest

E T Bell *Men of mathematics*, Simon and Schuster 1986

R Courant and H E Robbins *What is mathematics?*, Oxford University
Press (New York) 1941

M Kac and S Ulam *Mathematics and logic*, Penguin 1979

M Kraitchik *Mathematical recreations*, Dover

H Rademacher and O Toeplitz *The enjoyment of mathematics*, Princeton
1994 (also published by Dover)

Sherman K Stein *Mathematics: the man made universe*, McGraw-Hill 1976

Ian Stewart *The problems of mathematics*, Oxford University Press 1987
(reprinted as *From here to infinity*, Oxford University Press 1996)

Texts on specific mathematical topics

A Beiler *Recreations in the theory of numbers*, Dover 1964

R Courant *Differential and integral calculus* (2 volumes), Blackie 1934
(reprinted many times; later editions are by R Courant and F John,
published by Wiley)

H S M Coxeter *Introduction to geometry*, Wiley 1961

H Davenport *The higher arithmetic*, Cambridge University Press 1982 (also
published by Dover 1983)

I M Gelfand and A Shen *Algebra*, Birkhauser 1993

Ross Honsberger *Ingenuity in mathematics*, Mathematical Association of
America 1970
Mathematical gems, Mathematical Association of America 1973
(numerous other titles by the same author)

S Lang and G Morrow *Geometry: a high school course* Springer 1983

Z A Melzak *Invitation to geometry*, Wiley 1983

Ivan Niven *Numbers, rational and irrational*, Mathematical Association of
America 1961

N Ya Vilenkin *Combinatorics*, Academic Press 1971

A M Yaglom and I M Yaglom *Challenging mathematical problems with
elementary solutions* (2 volumes), Dover 1987

Leo Zippin *Uses of infinity*, Mathematical Association of America 1962

Appendix: UK JMO awards

The whole aim of the UK Junior Mathematical Olympiad (JMO) is to challenge, to stimulate and to encourage *large numbers* of youngsters. Thus all participants whose scripts show clear signs of mathematical ability receive a medal of some kind – Gold, Silver or Bronze. The proportions are not fixed, but depend on the quality of scripts received each year (which, in turn, depends on the accessibility, or otherwise, of that year's question paper!).

Many of those who take part have no previous experience of tackling such problems, or of presenting their solutions in the required way, so one should not be surprised if some exceptionally talented students pass more-or-less unnoticed. It is certainly true that many UK JMO Bronze medallists subsequently outperform many Silver and Gold medallists, so one should not take the implied ranking of the candidates too seriously. Our aim is to encourage. Feedback suggests strongly that, though the papers are tough, the experience of taking part does indeed inspire many students to aim higher than they otherwise might have done.

Each UK JMO script receives

- a mark 'a' out of 10 for Section A (= number of correct answers), and
- a mark 'b' out of 10 for Section B (where 0 and 1 indicate no attempt, or no serious attempt, 2 and 3 indicate some serious but unsuccessful attempts, and $N + 3$ indicates N complete solutions.)

The resulting marks (a, b) are ordered on the basis of the second 'b' coordinate: for example, $(2, 5) > (7, 4)$.

In the following list of medallists and their schools we use the abbreviations S, C, GS, HS, CS, JS to stand for School, College, Grammar School, High School, Comprehensive School and Junior School respectively.

UK JMO awards: 1995

There were eleven *Gold medallists* – three of whom were *Highly commended* (scoring $\geq$ (7, 8)), and eight of whom were *Commended* (scoring $\geq$ (4, 7)). There were also 44 *Silver medallists* (those scoring $\geq$ (2, 6)), and 107 *Bronze medallists* (those scoring $\geq$ (2, 5)).

Gold medallists

Highly commended
Edward Catmur   *Hinchley Wood S*
David Knipe   *Sullivan Upper S*
J P Sistenich   *Caldicott S*

Commended
J D Cranch   *Elizabeth C*
Christopher Cummins   *Our Lady of Sion S*
Thomas Dougherty   *St Paul's Prep S*
Andrew Fisher   *Milbourne Lodge*
Thaddeus Fulford-Jones   *St Paul's Prep S*
Rachel Holmes   *King's Hall S*
Qiang Kwong   *St Paul's Prep S*
G Williams   *Hoe Bridge S*

Silver medallists

Hazel Alcraft   *Stockport GS*
Ross Axe   *King Edward's Camp Hill Boys S*
M D Bayes   *Manchester GS*
Henry Bowen   *Dulwich C*
Jonathan Boyd   *Sullivan Upper S*
A Bridges   *Repton Prep S*
David Chow   *Clifton College Prep S*
Nicola Clay   *Baines S*
S W Coleman   *Eagle House S*
Natasha Condon   *Broxbourne S*
David Craven   *Bishop Vesey's GS*
Ben Duncan   *Queen Mary's GS, Walsall*
Simon Farnsworth   *Tiffin Boys S*
Alex Green   *Stancliffe Hall S*
Christopher Harris   *Tiffin Boys S*
David Hodge   *Torquay Boys GS*
S N Horsman   *HS of Glasgow*
Christopher Ingham   *King Edward's Camp Hill Boys S*
Zak Jarvis   *Swavesey Village C*
Nicholas Lindsay   *Tiffin Boys S*
Jonathan Lowndes   *Abberley Hall S*
John Mackay   *Firrhill HS*

Harry Mason   *Cirencester Deer Park S*
Andrew McVitty   *Sullivan Upper S*
Neil Mitchell   *St Bedes S*
Sarah Monroe   *James Allens Girls S*
Tony Neville   *Ilford County HS*
Chun Hwa Pang   *Tiffin Boys S*
C J Rayson   *Netherhall S*
Jo Richardson   *Bancrofts S*
Josh Robinson   *Ipswich S*
Jeremy Sadler   *University College S*
Niall Sayers   *Bristol GS*
Ben Scholl   *Royal GS, Newcastle*
V Sivapathasundaram   *Dulwich C*
Stuart Smith   *Bell Baxter HS*
Manuel Starr   *Wilsons S*
Graham Stratton   *Ailwyn CS*
Andrew Thomas   *Queen Mary's GS, Walsall*
Simon Thomas   *Kingston GS*
J Vickeridge   *Royal GS, Worcester*
Christopher Waudby   *Bearsden Academy*
Mark Woodward   *George Ward S*
Andrew Young   *Cotham GS*

Bronze medallists

Muntasir Ali   *Copleston HS*
Jane Anderson   *Dunfermline HS*
Rehaan Anjum   *Kingston GS*
Jacob Barlow   *King James S*
Thomas Barnet-Lamb   *St James Middle S*
Graham Bates   *Solihull S*
Douglas Benzie   *Dollar Academy*
Vanessa Beresford   *Ipswich HS*
Richard Blake   *Hartismere HS*
Philip Blakely   *Barnard Castle S*
Zillah Boraston   *Kendrick S*
George Bradt   *St Paul's Prep S*
Dominic Byrne   *Lincoln Christ's Hospital S*
Jemba Bull   *St Peter's S*
David Capps   *Wirral GS*
John Cassidy   *Dulwich C*
Ousheng Cheng   *Bishopbriggs HS*
Dominic Curran   *Judd S*

127

Peter Darch   *Bournemouth S*
Daniel Day   *Queen Elizabeth's Hospital*
Katie De Wit   *Kent C*
Chris Dowden   *Hereford Cathedral S*
Sandy Douglas   *George Watsons C*
Pippa Dudley   *Ladies C, Guernsey*
Rachel Elkins   *Bohunt S*
Roger Ellison   *Queen Mary's GS, Walsall*
Nicholas Epstein   *St Christopher's S*
Louise Ferguson   *Douglas Academy*
Matthew Fox   *Swavesey Village C*
Paul Gadd   *Royal Latin S*
David Gallagher   *Emmbrook S*
Tom Garnett   *Swavesey Village C*
Benjamin Gee   *Caldicott S*
Aron Gelbard   *St Paul's Prep S*
Paul Gilson   *Clifton College Prep S*
Anne-Lise Goddings   *Wycombe Abbey S*
Alexandra Griffiths   *Stratford Girls GS*
Oliver Gryce   *Hendon S*
J P Guyett   *Caldicott S*
Anousheh Haghdadi   *King Edward's HS, Birmingham*
Robin Hawkes   *Bedford Modern S*
Emma Heald   *St Paul's Girls S*
Greg Henson   *Royal GS, High Wycombe*
Cynthia Herman   *Newstead Wood S*
T J Hignett   *Dr Challoners GS*
Gemma Hindson   *King Edward's HS, Birmingham*
Laura Hough   *St Andrew's S*
Andrew Hunt   *Queen Elizabeth's Boys S*
Lawrence Hutchinson   *Torquay Boys GS*
Kester Jarvis   *Swavesey Village C*
Julia Johnson   *Dragon S*
Fleur Kilburn-Toppin   *Channing S*
Tom Koczwara   *Manchester GS*
T A D Leeming   *Caldicott S*
Antony Lewis   *Windlesham House S*
Christopher Lord   *Arnold S*
Sophie Lyon   *Taunton Prep S*
Will Macnair   *High Storrs S*
Ian Malone   *Sullivan Upper S*
Sam Marrs   *Largs Academy*
Tristan Marshall   *Tiffin Boys S*
Ian Martin   *Parkside Community C*

A Mason   *Royal GS, Guildford*
Anna McColl   *St Paul's Girls S*
S McNellis   *Royal GS, Worcester*
Philip Medcalf   *St Benedict's S*
Helen Miller   *Withington Girls S*
Andrew Mills   *Portora Royal S*
Claire Mitchell   *Sullivan Upper S*
Philip Morgan   *Judd S*
Simon Motz   *St Paul's Prep S*
Kathryn Muirhead   *Truro HS*
Richard Murphy   *Queen Elizabeth's GS, Wakefield*
Rebecca Naylor   *St Helen's S*
H Neish   *HS of Glasgow*
Peter Nelson   *Tavistock C*
Sarah Nicholson   *Dollar Academy*
T P Pan   *Summer Fields S*
T M Part   *Caldicott S*
Nadia Patel   *Leeds Girls HS*
Graham Phillips   *Kings Junior S, Ely*
Sophie Pinner   *Stratford Girls GS*
Andrew Ralls   *Whitgift S*
Christina Reynolds   *Wimbledon HS*
Claire Reynolds   *Sutton Coldfield Girls S*
Deborah Reynolds   *Perse S for Girls*
M S Richards   *Summer Fields S*
Oliver Rosenberg   *City of London S*
James Rosewarm   *Bournemouth S*
Amy Rothwell   *Aylesbury HS*
Geoffrey Scodie   *Queen Elizabeth's Boys S*
William Sedley   *Parkside Community C*
Shena Shah   *Haberdashers Askes Girls S*
Peter Smyth   *Queen Elizabeth's Boys S*
M Sorensen   *Royal GS, Worcester*
Hannah Stock   *John Masefield HS*
I J Taylor   *Monmouth S*
R Thompson   *Torquay Boys GS*
Sophie Traylen   *St Paul's Girls S*
Stefan Turner   *Bournemouth S*
Mary Tweedale   *Antrim GS*
James Walker   *St David's S*
Sarah Whitfield   *Haberdashers Askes Girls S*
Layla Whitworth   *Oxford HS*
A Young   *HS of Glasgow*
Hazel Younger   *George Watsons C*
Sarah Zambonini   *Stratford Girls HS*

UK JMO awards: 1994

There were six *Gold medallists* – one of whom was *Highly commended* (scoring (9, 9)), and five of whom were *Commended* (scoring ≥ (3, 6)). There were also thirteen *Silver medallists* (those scoring ≥ (3,5)), and 84 *Bronze medallists* (those scoring ≥ (3,4) or (1, 5)).

Gold medallists

Highly commended
Chiin-Zhe Tan   *St Paul's Prep S*

Commended
Andrew Bamford   *Mall S*
Stephen Egli   *King Edward's S, Stratford*
Kathryn Harrison   *St John's S, Marlborough*
Claire Martin   *Haberdashers Askes Girls S*
C D A Mattey   *Priory S, Banstead*

Silver medallists

Jonathan Amos   *Haling Park S*
Adam Butterworth   *Cheadle Hulme S*
D Elstein   *St Paul's S*
Matthew Harrison   *Windlesham House S*
Lisa Harvey   *James Allens Girls S*
Chihiro Morishima   *Notre Dame Senior S*
Andrew Robinson   *Tadcaster GS*
F M Salah   *Caldicott S*
Vicki Swan   *Royal HS*
Justin Thompson   *Lyndon Secondary S*
David Turner   *Stockport GS*
Hugh Venables   *Tiffin Boys S*
Jack Vickeridge   Royal GS, Worcester

Bronze medallists

Andrew Aldcroft   *King S, Macclesfield*
Naji Ashry   *City of London S*
Jennifer Austen   *Oxford HS*
Andrew Aylett   *Stradbroke HS*
Fiona Bell   *Newstead Wood S*
Howard Birks   *Stockport GS*
Ben Brettell   *Abingdon S*
Charlotte Broadie   *Wycombe Abbey S*
Mark Burden   *Swanmore Secondary S*
Julia Carter   *Manhood Community C*
Timothy Case   *Gravesend Boys GS*
Caroline Catmur   *Hinchley Wood S*
Edward Catmur   *Hinchley Wood S*

Christopher Chiswell   *Solihull S*
Jaya Choparia   *Channing S*
Bobby Christie   *Ampleforth C Junior S*
Stella Christofides   *Sutton HS*
Anna Cocheme   *St Paul's Girls S*
Micha Colombo   *Oxford HS*
D Critchley   *Queen Elizabeth's GS, Blackburn*
Jennifer Davie   *Madras C*
Simon Davies   *Abingdon S*
Nevil Deane   *Dulwich C*
Helen Dixon   *Newcastle Church HS*
Neil Donaldson   *Madras C*
L Duncan   *Sevenoaks S*
Tom Fayle   *Torquay Boys GS*
Melanie Fiander   *North London Collegiate S*
David Gallagher   *Emmbrook S*
Melissa Gardner   *North London Collegiate S*
Ian Gasgoine   *Hitchin Boys S*
A G Gelbard   *St Paul's Prep S*
Huw Griffiths   *Haling Park S*
Jack Grover   *Royal GS, High Wycombe*
Alastair Hall   *Hazelwood S*
Anthony Hawkins   *Merchiston Castle S*
Piers Henderson   *Lewes Priory S*
Sam Henderson   *St Paul's Prep S*
M Henshall   *Royal GS, Worcester*
Edward Hicks   *St Bedes S, Redhill*
Robert Hoey   *Wolborough Hill S*
Ben Huckvale   *St Laurence S*
Jon Killingley   *Twyford S*
David Knipe   *Sullivan Upper S*
Jack Kuipers   *Dulwich C*
Richard Little   *St Albans S*
Peter Lumsdaine   *University College S*
Rosie Marsh   *Haberdashers Askes Girls S*
J D Marsters   *King Edward's S, Birmingham*
Paul Martin   *Dean Close Junior S*
Elizabeth McBrien   *Notre Dame Senior S*
Ellen Mogo   *Bromley HS*
Ralph Owen   *Queen Elizabeth's Hospital*
Christopher Pearson   *Arden S*
James Percival   *Woodbridge HS*

Christopher Purcell   *King Edward's S, Bath*
Nabeel Rauf   *King Edward's Camp Hill Boys S*
Ben Read   *Simon Balle S*
Alex Rinsler   *Shrewsbury S*
Ben Ritchie   *Wolborough Hill S*
Samuel Roberts   *Dulwich C*
E Ryder   *Berkhamsted S*
H M Shepherd   *Queen Elizabeth's GS, Wakefield*
Tamlin Simpson   *Bottisham Village C*
J P Sistenich   *Caldicott S*
V Siva   *Dulwich C*
Tim Smith   *City of London S*
Charles Stedman   *St Paul's Prep S*
M J Stevenson   *Bradford GS*
Jonathan Stewart   *Highgate JS*

Alexander Summers   *Priory HS, Exeter*
Stephen Talbot   *Royal GS, Newcastle*
Alex Thom   *Copthorne S*
Mahmut Tuncer   *King Edward's Camp Hill Boys S*
Richard Watts   Comberton Village C
Annette Weir   *Hutchesons GS*
Ben Whately   *Windlesham House S*
Jennifer Whitehouse   *Bredon Hill Middle S*
Stephen Willey   *St George's S*
Antonia Williams   *Wycombe Abbey S*
Gareth Williams   *Hoe Bridge S*
Katie Wollerton   *Badminton S*
Andrew Young   *Cotham GS*
Peter Young   *Mall S*

UK JMO awards: 1993

There were nine *Gold medallists* – one of whom was *Highly commended* (scoring (7, 9)), and eight of whom were *Commended* (scoring ≥ (4, 7) or (8, 6)). There were also 35 *Silver medallists* (those scoring ≥ (3, 6) or (7, 5)), and 152 *Bronze medallists* (those scoring ≥ (2, 5) or (6, 4)).

Gold medallists

Highly commended
Gavin Winston   *Royal GS, High Wycombe*

Commended
David Allan   *Dulwich C*
Jonathan Foster   *St Laurence S*
Simon Frankau   *Wycliffe C*
Philip Howard   *Kings College S, Wimbledon*
Adrian Sanders   *Kings College S, Wimbledon*
Bennet Summers   *St Paul's S*
Ian Thatcher   *Manshead S*
Thomas Voice   *Comberton Middle S*

Silver medallists

M A Ackroyd   *Monmouth S*
N R Aldridge   *Latymer Upper S*
Thomas Bailey   *Winchester C*

A S Bell   *St Olaves GS*
Oliver Boney   *Winchester C*
Michael C Ching   *Oundle S*
Peter Corbett   *Ranelagh S*
Iain Crouch   *Hutchesons GS*
James Cunnington   *King Edward's S, Birmingham*
Angela Ditchfield   *King Edward's HS, Birmingham*
Iain Flockhart   *St Bedes S*
Toby Gee   *Frome Community C*
Sunpreet Grewal   *Forest S*
Anna Hawkins   *Ranelagh S*
K Hayward-Bradley   *Rugby S*
Paul Johnston   *Manchester GS*
Richard Keane   *Yateley S*
Nicholas Kennedy   *Queen Elizabeth's Hospital*
Georg Klein   *Vienna International S*
Oliver Lan   *Haberdashers Askes S*
Jonathan Lee   *St Paul's Prep S*

Stephen Paul   *Haberdashers Askes S*
E K Poon   *Berkhamsted S*
Claire Postlethwaite   *Tonbridge Girls GS*
Chris Rayment   *Warden Park S*
Paul Russell   *St Brides HS*
Amit Shah   *Haberdashers Askes S*
R M Stewart   *Trinity S*
Matthew Steynor   *Royal GS, Guildford*
Chiin-Zhe Tan   *St Paul's Prep S*
Jane Toohe   *Sir William Perkins S*
Matthew Watts   *Royal GS, Guildford*
Alice Welham   *Clifton C*
Robert Whittaker   *Bredon Hill Middle S*
Philip Yeo   *St Andrews HS*

Bronze medallists

Alex Aiken   *Westminster S*
Lucy Algeo   *James Allens Girls S*
Richard Alexander   *Madras C*
R Allen   *King Edward's Camp Hill Boys S*
D S Anderson-Burley   *Charterhouse*
Louise Asher   *Dame Alice Owen's S*
Hai Yuen Aw   *King Edward's S, Birmingham*
G R Ayre   *Monmouth S*
T S Bagot   *Rugby S*
Colin Ball   *King Edward's S, Birmingham*
Andrew Bamford   *Mall S*
Linda Bell   *Haberdashers Askes Girls S*
James Beale   *Clifton C*
William Bentley   *Droitwich HS*
Mark Bicknell   *Woolmer Hill S*
Gordon Black   *Golspie HS*
Lorraine Blacker   *Tadcaster GS*
Joseph Bootle   *Durrington HS*
Gary Bosworth   *Oundle S*
Cennydd Bowles   *Shrewsbury S*
R J Brown   *St Birinus S*
Allan Bruce   *Elgin Academy*
David Buse   *Formby HS*
Robert Cardno   *Oldmachar Academy*
Michael Carse   *Highfield S*
George Carty   *Belmont CS*
Victor Chan   *Westerminster S*
Andrea Charleton   *Newstead Wood S*
Yemon Choi   *Westminster S*
Anil Chouksey   *Manchester GS*
Juliette Chrisman   *Millais S*
Mark Coghlan   *Sullivan Upper S*
Gregory Cook   *St Olaves GS*
Philip Cooper   *Harrogate GS*
Ben Corlett   *Ffynone House S*

Christopher Coulbeck   *Bancrofts S*
Christian Coulson   *Westminster S*
Philip Cowans   *Colchester Royal GS*
John Craven   *Colonel Frank Seely CS*
Matthew Craven   *Sir Roger Manwoods S*
Ashley Cunnington   *Queen Mary's GS*
Ruth Curran   *Parrs Wood HS*
Douglas Currie   *Elgin Academy*
Reena Davda   *James Allens Girls S*
Mary-Ann Davies   *Dean Close S*
Matthew Daws   *Northampton Boys S*
Daniel Douglas   *Longridge HS*
Peter d'Souza   *Stockport GS*
Charles Economou   *St Paul's Prep S*
J Edgcombe   *Perse S*
Terence Ferguson   *Ridgeway S*
Charles Finch   *Loughborough S*
Patrick Finglass   *King Edward's S, Birmingham*
Emma Firth   *Bury Girls GS*
Kerran Fisher   *Taunton S*
Steven Fitzgerald   *Harrogate GS*
Daniel Fleeton   *St Patricks GS*
J Fozard   *Lancaster Royal GS*
William Garrood   *British S of Brussels*
David Gatrell   *Manchester GS*
Christopher Gibbs   *King Edward's S,*
     Birmingham
Ruth Green   *Holmes Chapel CS*
Daniel Griffith   *Bedford S*
D L Griffith-Jones   *Bishops Stortford College JS*
Nicholas Hamilton   *Dulwich C*
Kathryn Harrison   *Marlborough C*
Emily Hayes   *Berkhamsted Girls S*
R Heslop   *Richmond S*
Ian Hill   *Bury Boys GS*
Christopher Hill   *Repton S*
Mark Hird   *Queen Elizabeth GS, Wakefield*
Duncan Hodges   *Huish Episcopi S*
Karen Hodges   *John Kyrle HS*
Tony Hodson   *King Edward's S, Birmingham*
Pippa Hopkins   *Chelmsford HS*
Stephen Houghton   *Royal GS, Worcester*
Gethin Huckle   *Sir William Borlases GS*
Zosia Huk   *Forest S*
Tom Hutchings   *Ashcombe S*
P A Kanapathipillai   *Chigwell S*
J S Kennedy   *Winchester C*
Deborah Kong   *Haberdashers Askes Girls S*
Jeffrey Leung   *St Andrews RC S*
Paul Levy   *Merchant Taylors S*
Iain Leverett   *Bishops Stortford C*
Jonathan Linkins   *Wilmslow HS*

L B Living   *Oundle S*
Samuel Macdonald   *Forest S*
O W Marsland   *Nottingham HS*
D L J Martin   *Oundle S*
Sithu Win Maung   *Royal GS, Newcastle*
Peter le May   *Hampton S*
Keith Miles   *Whitgift S*
Mark Miller   *Bedford S*
Sarah Miller   *Davenant Foundation S*
Phyroze Mohamed   *Bury Boys GS*
Allan Morley   *St Georges C*
Christopher Morris   *Lady Manners S*
Richard Neill   *Wellington C*
K Nickell   *Oxford HS*
Marion Palles-Clark   *Kendrick S*
Alice Park   *James Allens Girls S*
Brendan Payne   *Dr Challoners GS*
Stephen Pearce   *Millfield S*
Amanda Peppercorn   *Marlborough C*
Timothy Perutz   *Huntingdon S*
Colin Phipps   *Bristol GS*
Matthew Piatkus   *Haberdashers Askes S*
Juliet Ponsonby   *St Swithuns S*
Jonathan Potts   *Haberdashers Askes S*
D A Price   *Royal GS, Worcester*
Kabr Pruthi   *Westminster S*
M Robbins   *Warwick S*
Simon Robinson   *Latymer Upper S*
Marc Sanders   *Latymer Upper S*
Chris Sayers   *Millfield S*
Thomas Schofield   *Roundwood Park S*
Vikas Shah   *Heathland S*
A C N Singleton   *Oundle S*
Daniel Siva   *St Paul's S*

Robert Smith   *Windsor Boys S*
William Snell   *Clifton C*
Edward Snelson   *Portsmouth GS*
S C Speed   *Whitgift S*
Murali Sri-Ganeshan   *Dulwich C*
Jonathan Stevens   *Winchester C*
Richard Stockfis   *Manchester GS*
R Stollery   *Ipswich S*
Philip Sumner   *Holy Trinity S*
V Tattersall   *Bolton S Girls Division*
John Taylor   *St Gregory's HS*
W Thorne   *Winchester C*
T Tibbits   *Winchester C*
Ruth Tolan   *Parrs Wood HS*
Jonathan Tricker   *Judd S*
Robert Truswell   *Woldgate S*
David Tucker   *Whitgift S*
Timothy Underwood   *Trinity S*
Ian Wallace   *Bedford S*
Colin Watson   *Our Lady & St Patrick's C*
Rowland Webb   *Dulwich C*
James Wells   *Judd S*
Elizabeth Wenham   *Dean Close S*
David White   *Holmes Chapel CS*
Mark Whitehouse   *King Edward's S, Birmingham*
Martin Whittaker   *Wolverhampton GS*
Matthew Wicks   *Kings College S, Wimbledon*
Andrew Williams   *St Christopher S*
Tom Wood   *Lancaster Royal GS*
Mark Woolston   *Sherborne S*
Michelle Young   *Aylesbury HS*
Eric Yu   *Leighton Park S*

UK JMO awards: 1992

There were ten *Gold medallists* – three of whom were *Highly commended* (scoring (7, 10)), and seven of whom were *Commended* (scoring ≥ (7, 8) or (8, 7) or (10, 6)). There were also 34 *Silver medallists* (those scoring ≥ (8, 5) or (5, 6)), and 128 *Bronze medallists* (those scoring ≥ (7, 4) or (3, 5)).

Gold medallists

Highly commended
Richard Edlin   *Westminster S*
Julian Huppert   *Perse S*
Hugh Robinson   *King Henry VIII S*

Commended
Michael Anderson   *Royal GS, Guildford*
Neville Eisenberg   *Haberdashers Askes S*
Timothy Hawkins   *Malvern C*
Andrew Holland   *Solihull S*
Daniel Sacks   *City of London S*
Paul Thomas   *Wellington S*
Uri Zarfaty   *City of London S*

Silver medallists

T E Alden   *King Edward's S, Birmingham*
B D Ashforth   *Bedford S*
T S Bagot   *Caldicott S*
Kevin Baker   *Queen Elizabeth's Hospital*
Mark Boyd   *Stockport GS*
Francis Brown   *Eton C*
J M Burley   *Caldicott S*
Robert Butler   *Caldicott S*
George Carty   *Belmont CS*
Ashley Cunnington   *Queen Mary's GS*
Alex Evans   *Westminster S*
David Evans   *Clifton C*
James Fletcher   *Winchester C*
David Flowerdew   *Impington Village C*
G Foot   *Clifton C*
John Haselgrave   *King Henry VIII S*
James Humpherson   *Harry Carlton S*
Peter Keevash   *Leeds GS*
Stephen Kirkman   *St Paul's S*
Simon Lewis   *St Peter's CE HS*
Diarmid Mackenzie   *King Edward's S, Birmingham*
R G Metcalf   *Winchester C*
D S Ratnayake   *Merchant Taylors S*

C Rhodes   *City of London S*
David Riley   *St George's C*
Edward Robinson   *Winchester C*
Douglas Sharp   *Stewarts Melville C*
David Simon   *Shrewsbury S*
Geoffrey Simons   *Cheltenham C*
David Tait   *Hutchesons GS*
Colin Watson   *Our Lady & St Patrick's C*
Ben Winhall   *Wellington S*
Guy Winkworth   *Winchester C*
Michael Yoong   *Winchester C*

Bronze medallists

Sunil Adwani   *Stewarts Melville C*
David Allan   *Dulwich C*
Sarah Allatt   *Haberdashers Askes Girls S*
John Allister   *Stockport GS*
Helena Ancock   *Kings S, Canterbury*
Edward Anderson   *Dulwich C*
Stuart Anderson   *Kings S, Taunton*
Joe Appleby   *St Edward's S, Oxford*
T H Ashton   *Westminster S*
Ross Avery   *Tonbridge S*
Amitava Banerjee   *Hymers C*
Kerri Bates   *Balfron HS*
Josh Bell   *City of London S*
Tom Bentham   *Lancaster Royal GS*
M Bhattacharyya   *Haberdashers Askes Girls S*
Helen Bicknell   *Aylesbury HS*
Suman Biswas   *Kings College S, Wimbledon*
Emma Blake   *Penair S*
A J Block   *Winchester C*
Aiden Bowes   *Clifton C*
Mike Broadwish   *Haberdashers Askes S*
Richard Brown   *Kings College S, Wimbledon*
Mark Byers   *Queen Mary's GS*
James Carroll   *Manchester GS*
Francis Chambers   *Kendrick S*
R J Cheesman   *Kings College S, Wimbledon*
Bethany Collins   *North London Collegiate S*
Philip Corser   *Winchester C*
Jonathan Crown   *Brighton C*

J A Cunnington   *King Edward's S, Birmingham*
Jane Currie   *Herts & Essex HS*
T B McFarland Davidson   *Kings S, Macclesfield*
Helen Deacon   *Tormead S*
Ben Delucchi   *Malbank S*
Rajat Dhar   *Gordonstoun S*
Kenneth Eames   *Judd S*
G Edwards   *Tonbridge S*
Paul Emery   *Dr Challoners GS*
J H W Enthoven   *Eton C*
Andrew Fargus   *Millfield S*
N J Fielding   *Shrewsbury S*
David Firth   *Castle S*
Tom Fitzgerald   *Yardley Court C*
A D Foxcroft   *Bishops Stortford C*
David Gatrell   *Manchester GS*
Alison Mary Girling   *Licensed Victuallers S*
George Gorringe   *Colchester Royal GS*
Nicholas Harmer   *Royal GS, Guildford*
Simon Hedley   *Tonbridge S*
Alice Henchley   *James Allens Girls S*
N Higginbottom   *Abingdon S*
Matthew Hodgson   *Perse S*
S Hodson   *Marlborough C*
C T Hui   *Lancing C*
H Hunt   *Oxford HS*
Jonathan Isaby   *Kings College S, Wimbledon*
Marcus Jones   *Winchester C*
Wesley Jones   *Sandbach S*
Claire Jordan   *Croydon HS*
Eleanor Joslin   *St John's S*
Susan Kennedy   *Sullivan Upper S*
Guy King   *Foyle & Londonderry C*
Deborah Kong   *Haberdashers Askes Girls S*
O J Kunc   *Bradford GS*
Karen Lai   *Sutton HS*
Aron Lazarus   *City of London S*
Gary Lloyd   *South Hunsley S*
Theo Lorenc   *Ralph Allen S*
Catherine Macdonald   *Portsmouth HS*
Hugh Maddison   *Wellington C*
G Markham   *Winchester C*
Tom Marsh   *Oundle S*
Douglas Mattison   *Manchester GS*
Helen McDaniel   *Collegiate GS*
P J McKean   *Bishops Stortford C*
Rowan Medhurst   *Queens S, Taunton*
Christopher Mellor   *Parrs Wood HS*
Joel Meyer   *Royal GS, High Wycombe*

Mervyn Myles   *Perth HS*
Jeffrey Neate   *King Edward's Camp Hill Boys S*
R J Neill   *Caldicott S*
Edward O'Malley   *Ampleforth C*
A Paleit   *Abingdon S*
Ryuk Park   *Frankfurt International S*
Douglas Pendse   *Dr Challoners GS*
S J Preston   *King Edward's S, Birmingham*
T W Pullen   *Tiffin Boys S*
Edward Ratzer   *Eton C*
Chris Rayment   *Warden Park S*
Daniel Rees   *Christs C, Brecon*
I Richards   *Canford S*
Clare Ridgeway   *Portsmouth HS*
Jonathan Ridgway   *Wycliffe C*
Michael Roberts   *Royal GS, High Wycombe*
Thomas Robinson   *Manchester GS*
Jonathan Rudoe   *Haberdashers Askes S*
J Saldhana   *Dulwich C*
Sam Sandiford   *Yardley Court S*
Catherine Saunders   *Berkhamsted Girls S*
Peter Fane Saunders   *Ampleforth C*
C Sayer   *Oxford HS*
Neil Shepherd   *Friends S, Lisburn*
M Shilton   *Ampleforth C*
Jalin Somaiya   *Winchester C*
Andrew Smith   *Queen Mary's GS*
Adam Stearns   *Eton C*
Sara Stewart   *Collegiate GS*
Rachel Sunderland   *Holmes Chapel CS*
Lee Tsang Tan   *Dulwich C*
Christopher Towell   *Penrice S*
M D Tyler   *Bishops Stortford C*
Simon Waddington   *Bedford S*
Alexander Walsh   *Winchester C*
Julia Warren   *Ipswich HS*
Jo Watkins   *Aylesbury HS*
James Wells   *Judd S*
Kate Went   *Sullivan Upper S*
Pippa Whitehouse   *Sutton HS*
Paul Whittaker   *Woodhey HS*
Anthony Williams   *Abingdon S*
Hywel Williams   *Crickhowell HS*
Ben Wood   *Bury Boys GS*
Jerome Workman   *Wilnecote HS*
Michael Yates   *Manchester GS*
Patrick Yates   *Lancing C*
Lai Cheng Yew   *City of London Girls S*
David Zucarotti   *Eastbourne C*

UK JMO awards: 1991

There were fifteen *Gold medallists* – six of whom were *Highly commenced* (scoring (7, 9) or (9, 8)), and nine of whom were *Commended* (scoring ≥ (5, 9) or (6, 8) or (7, 7)). There were also 42 *Silver medallists* (those scoring ≥ (4, 8) or (5, 7) or (6, 6)), and 122 *Bronze medallists* (those scoring ≥ (3, 6) or (4, 5) or (5, 4)).

Gold medallists

Highly commended

Duncan Archer   *Yarm S*
Matthew Fayers   *Wilsons S*
S K Gardiner   *Sedbergh S*
Ben Green   *Fairfield GS*
Ben Hutchings   *Ashcombe S*
Hugh Robinson   *King Henry VIII S*

Commended

C D Anderson   *Tonbridge S*
Michael Anderson   *Royal GS, Guildford*
Julian Bean   *St Paul's S*
Gawain Bosworth   *Nottingham HS*
Edward Crane   *Colchester Royal GS*
Richard Davies   *Dulwich C*
Ian Kent   *King Edward's S, Birmingham*
Jeremy Large   *Winchester C*
S J Lucas   *St Olaves GS*

Silver medallists

A D Barnes   *Yardley Court S*
Alex Bowley   *Nottingham HS*
Stephen Chewten   *Tonbridge S*
Ben Coppock   *Dr Challoners GS*
S Essen   *Kings College S, Wimbledon*
Naomi Farr   *King Edward's HS, Birmingham*
Jonathan Foy   *Windlesham House S*
Nicholas Harmer   *Royal GS, Guildford*
Suzie Havard   *Haberdashers Askes Girls S*
Andrew Hennessy   *Millfield S*
Stephen Hodson   *Marlborough C*
J E M Horth   *Ampleforth C*
David Hunt   *Perse S*
C J D Johnson   *Winchester C*
C P Johnston   *Warwick S*
Jonathan Jordan   *High Storrs S*
Thomas Kan   *Kings College S, Wimbledon*
Peter Keevash   *Leeds GS*
Jonathan Kirkpatrick   *Winchester C*
Christoph Krammer   *Vienna International S*

Daniel Lambourne   *Royal GS, High Wycombe*
Ian MacMullen   *Durham Johnston CS*
P J McKean   *Bishops Stortford College JS*
James Muir   *Royal GS, Guildford*
John-Mark Mullen   *Wallace HS*
Ben Noakes   *Loughborough GS*
A Pavlovich   *Abingdon S*
Matthew Peakman   *Millfield S*
Lucy Porter   *Bath HS*
Martin Read   *Durrington HS*
Christophe Rhodes   *City of London S*
T M Rooke   *Hereford Cathedral S*
D P Sanders   *Chesterton Community C*
Kevin Sawers   *Colchester Royal GS*
Christopher Tolman   *Trinity S*
R Vann   *St Paul's S*
Wo Wai-Man   *Underhill Prep S*
Colin Watson   *Our Lady & St Patrick's C*
William Whittow   *Dr Challoners GS*
N R Wilson   *Shrewsbury S*
T Womack   *Winchester C*
Charles Yorke   *Bedford S*

Bronze medallists

E Achucooro   *Ardingly College JS*
Jayanth Arnold   *Winchester C*
David Bailey   *Nottingham HS*
Vivien Bailey   *Trinity S*
Kevin Baker   *Queen Elizabeth's Hospital*
S A Ballard   *Wilsons S*
S Balls   *Trinity S*
Richard Bannister   *Shrewsbury S*
F Baron   *Dulwich C*
Peter Beresford   *Roundwood Park S*
Neville Blackburn   *Worle S*
Greg Bostow   *Ashlyns S*
Sonya Branch   *Ardingly College JS*
James Brooks   *Wellington S*
James Buddell   *Bishops Stortford C*
David Cameron   *Millfield S*
Coralie Carle   *Bath HS*
Rupak Chandra   *Dr Challoners GS*

Antony Clarke   *Ardingly College JS*

Christopher Clark   *Lady Lumleys S*

Neil Coffey   *North Halifax HS*

H L S Collet   *Winchester C*

Bethany Collins   *North London Collegiate S*

Daniel Crewe   *Ipswich S*

Caroline Cracknell   *France Hill S*

D A Curtis   *Merchant Taylors S*

Mackenzie Dallas   *Uppingham S*

R Daniel   *Warwick S*

Elizabeth Darwin   *St Paul's Girls S*

Timothy Dawes   *Charterhouse*

Richard Dewire   *High Storrs S*

Andrew Eakins   *Queen Elizabeth's HS, Hexham*

David Easto   *Friary S*

Richard Edwards   *Hinchingbrooke S*

J R Elliot   *Winchester C*

Adrian Eyre   *Winston Churchill S*

Susanna Flett   *City of London Girls S*

P A L Foster   *Repton S*

Jonathan Fowler   *Simon Langton GS*

B Fuller   *Queen Elizabeth's GS, Blackburn*

J Gair   *Royal GS, Newcastle*

Daniel Glenn   *Thetford GS*

A Godfrey   *St Anselm's S*

Jonathan Goldstone   *Manchester GS*

C R Greenhill   *Tonbridge S*

Ian Greig   *Dulwich C*

M Grimwade   *Kings S, Peterborough*

Kevin Heath   *St George's C*

Jesse Hershkowitz   *Westminster S*

J Higgin   *St Paul's S*

Andrew Holland   *Solihull S*

James Howarth   *King Edward's S, Birmingham*

Mark Howarth   *Lancing C*

Andrew Howman   *Notre Dame HS*

Neil Hughes   *Hereford Cathedral S*

Robin Hutt   *Manchester GS*

Christopher Jones   *Yardley Court S*

Nicholas Jeffryes   *Tonbridge S*

James Jennings   *West Somerset Community S*

Mark Kawakita   *Royal GS, High Wycombe*

G Kershaw   *Winchester C*

Denise Kong   *Haberdashers Askes Girls S*

Joyce Kwong   *Malvern Girls S*

Pippa Lam   *Aylesbury HS*

Jonathan Lawn   *Sedbergh S*

B Lewis   *Manchester GS*

Mark Lewis   *King Edward's S, Birmingham*

John Ling   *Wellington S*

Lok-Tin Ma   *Highgate Junior S*

Howard Martin   *Kings S, Peterborough*

Kirsty McCaw   *Bath HS*

Alison McLean   *Wallace HS*

Ewan McPherson   *Balerno High S*

Ben Meadows   *Yardley Court S*

Susie Merick   *Brighton & Hove HS*

T C Montagu-Smith   *Westminster S*

Robert Moretto   *Royal GS, High Wycombe*

A P Morrell   *Westminster S*

Peter Morrish   *Dr Challoners GS*

H Morrison   *Norwich S*

Ambrose Nankivell   *Shenley Court S*

J D Nicholl   *Wellington C*

Neal O'Connor   *King Edward's S, Birmingham*

Peter O'Donovan   *Brighton C*

Deri O'Regan   *Davenant Foundation*

Louisa Orton   *Ipswich HS*

Philip Outram   *Marlborough C*

Andrew Partridge   *Pemberton S*

Heidi Peile   *Aylesbury HS*

David Peilow   *Queens C, Taunton*

Jennifer Phillips   *Haberdashers Askes Girls S*

Philip Pope   *Dr Challoners GS*

Brian Quinlon   *Castle S*

Tim Raby   *Perse S*

Nicholas Redman   *Conyers S*

Douglas Robson   *Nottingham HS*

David Root   *Loughborough GS*

S J Sandiford   *Yardley Court S*

Ashley Sarangi   *Repton S*

Jessica Sharp   *Aylesbury HS*

A Sheffield   *Tonbridge S*

Neil Shepherd   *Friends S, Lisburn*

Robert Sheridan   *Dulwich C*

John Shore   *Royal GS, High Wycombe*

Jennifer Siggers   *Kings HS for Girls*

J M Sinclair   *Winchester C*

Graham Spenceley   *Kingston GS*

Rebecca Spencer   *Friary S*

J P Stacey   *Queen Elizabeth's GS, Blackburn*

Lee-Tsang Tan   *Dulwich C*

Vincent Tang   *Westminster S*

Rosemary Taylor   *St Martin's S*

Ben Tregenna   *Poltair S*

Matthew Tyler   *Bishops Stortford College JS*

R J Vine   *Shrewsbury S*

Ben Walker   *Kings S, Peterborough*

Adam Wardell   *Wellington S*

Mary Wenham   *Dean Close S*

Michael Williams   *Stewarts Melville C*

Tristan Wilson   *Royal GS, Guildford*

Victor Yu   *Malmesbury S*

Uri Zarfaty   *City of London S*

UK JMO awards: 1990

There were 26 *Gold medallists* – twelve of whom were *Highly commended* (scoring (5, 10) or (7, 8) or (8, 6) or (9, 5)), and fourteen of whom were *Commended* (scoring ≥ (5, 7) or (6, 6) or (8, 4) or (9, 3)). There were also 73 *Silver medallists* (those scoring ≥ (2, 8) or (3, 7) or (4, 5) or (6, 4) or (7, 2)), and 181 *Bronze medallists* (those scoring ≥ (1, 7) or (2, 5) or (3, 4) or (4, 3) or (5, 2) or (7, 1)).

Gold medallists

Highly commended

David Bamford   *Arnold S*
Mathew Cordell   *Woolmer Hill S*
Jeremy Fagan   *King Edward's S, Birmingham*
Nicholas Forbes   *St John's S*
Edmund Green   *Abraham Darby S*
Gideon Greenspan   *City of London S*
Ben Hutchings   *Ashcombe S*
Luke Pebody   *Lawrence Sheriff S*
Adam Pushkin   *King Edward's S, Birmingham*
Michael Romose   *Uppingham S*
David Root   *Loughborough GS*
Judith Stone   *Perse S for Girls*

Commended

Mark Ainsworth   *Dr Challoners GS*
Richard Bates   *Solihull S*
S Curtis   *Royal GS, Newcastle*
Richard Davies   *Dulwich C*
Charles Dreyer   *Winchester C*
R A Haken   *Hurstpierpoint C*
Graham Hazel   *Chesterton Community C*
J Heritage   *St Paul's S*
S Jacobsberg   *Perse S for Girls*
Andrew Ker   *King Edward's S, Birmingham*
Nicholas Morgan   *Trinity S*
Danny Squier   *Kingswood S*
Timothy Ward   *Abingdon S*
P Waterfall   *Millfield S*

Silver medallists

S V Balls   *Trinity S*
A Bardos   *Herts & Essex HS*
P Barnes   *Dr Challoners GS*
A Bennett   *Kings S, Macclesfield*
P Molyneux Berry   *Clifton C*
S Bolton   *City of London Girls S*
C Bowles   *St Christopher's S*
K Bramham   *Skipton Girls HS*
J Britnell   *Durham Johnston CS*
C Bysouth   *Roseberry S*
W Chiang   *Dean Close S*
J Clark   *Chelmsford Community HS*
G Clemo   *Atherstone S*
A Critchley   *Bolton S Girls Division*
N Cross   *Kent C*
S Davidson   *Richard Hale S*
N Davies   *Solihull S*
T Dennis   *Kings S, Peterborough*
M Devereux   *Hereford Cathedral S*
C Dickson   *Yarm S*
T Dilworth   *Dulwich C*
A Disley   *Edlington Community S*
M Ferguson   *Royal GS, Guildford*
R Fitzhugh   *Shrewsbury S*
J Fowlston   *Winchester C*
C Gingell   *Chesham HS*
F Goodwillie   *Oakham S*
B Green   *Fairfield GS*
L Hartley   *Sutton Coldfield Girls S*
J Hasson   *Allertonshire S*
M Hawke   *Haberdashers Askes Girls S*
J Hill   *Winchester C*
E Hodby   *Oxford HS*
D Holtom   *Royal GS, Guildford*
E Horsfall   *Haydon Bridge HS*
J Irving   *Whitgift S*
L Jordinson   *Arnold S*
O Keenan   *Kings S, Peterborough*
B Kipling   *Kings S, Grantham*
M Kirk   *Dr Challoners GS*
D Kong   *Haberdashers Askes Girls S*
N Lewis   *Aylesbury HS*
R Lochead   *Solihull S*
J M Lochmann   *Winchester C*
I Luck   *Guilsborough S*
A J Lynch   *Winchester C*

I MacMullen   *Durham Johnston CS*
D Martin   *Madras C*
S Mayes   *Glyn S*
N Morphet   *Prudhoe HS*
J Nash   *Shrewsbury S*
N O'Connor   *King Edward's Camp Hill Boys S*
P O'Donovan   *St Christopher's S*
J Peat   *Park View CS*
M Phillips   *Winchester C*
P Phillips   *Winchester C*
J Reynolds   *Norwich S*
A Royal   *Boston GS*
J de Sa   *Royal GS, Newcastle*
S Scott   *Elgin Academy*
C Shaw   *Oakham S*
J Slabbert   *Dean Close S*
J Smith   *Loughborough GS*
S Smith   *Dulwich C*
E Stacey   *Clifton C*
N Stones   *Solihull S*
G Thomas   *Hereford Cathedral S*
C Thomson   *Winchester C*
D Wallace   *Bedford S*
R Warren   *Ipswich HS*
A Wells   *Sutton Coldfield Girls S*
J Westbury   *City of London S*
L P Wyszinski   *King Edward's Camp Hill Boys S*

Bronze medallists

C Allen   *Bishopshalt S*
P Andrew   *Queen Elizabeth's GS*
N Anderson   *Sullivan Upper S*
D Archer   *Yarm S*
G Atkins   *Farnham Heath End S*
R J Baggaley   *Nottingham HS*
J Baker   *St Bedes S*
M Barnes   *Kings S, Peterborough*
J Barrett   *King Edward's S, Birmingham*
S Bell   *Clifton C*
G Berry   *Dr Challoners GS*
R Berry   *King Edward's HS, Birmingham*
M Bordewitch   *Shrewsbury S*
A Boyce   *Boston GS*
R Boyd   *King Edward's HS, Birmingham*
D Brook   *St Paul's S*
T Brooker   *Allertonshire S*
J D Brooks   *Wellington S*
M J Brown   *Dulwich C*
D J Burton   *Millfield S*
S Cantney   *Rathmore GS*
S Carr   *Hinchingbroke S*
C Carter   *Herts & Essex HS*

D J W Cash   *Hampton S*
M E Cinnamond   *Sullivan Upper S*
G Chandra   *Bolton S Girls Division*
D Chantler   *Sullivan Upper S*
E Clarke   *Carisbrooke HS*
J Cobb   *Churchfields S*
H Cocker   *Bath HS*
N Coffey   *North Halifax HS*
M Coles   *Clifton C*
J Couling   *Loughborough GS*
D Cran   *Sullivan Upper S*
R Crawley   *Langley Park Boys S*
D Crosby   *Carisbrooke HS*
H Cross   *Abbeylands S*
S J Cross   *Nottingham HS*
D Crossley   *King Edward's S, Birmingham*
A Cumming   *Repton Prep S*
S Cunningham   *St Gergory's S*
D T Darley   *Caterham S*
S Dassanayake   *Bishopshalt S*
M Davis   *Royal GS, High Wycombe*
J Dawson   *Kings S, Bruton*
S Daykin   *Little Heath S*
M Dillon   *St Louis GS*
P G Dixon   *Lord Wandsworth C*
E Dodgson   *Hulme Girls GS*
M Dolphin   *Comberton Middle S*
M T J Early   *Whitgift S*
A Edwards   *Abingdon S*
C Evans   *King Edward's S, Aston*
J Ferro   *Dulwich C*
S Folwell   *Nottingham HS*
P A L Foster   *Repton Prep S*
S Fox   *King Edward's S, Stratford*
A Freer   *Minster S*
B Fuggles   *Abingdon S*
B Fuller   *Queen Elizabeth's GS*
S Glenwright   *Queen Elizabeth's Hospital*
M Godber   *Royal Latin S*
N K Goh   *Winchester C*
M Goodfellow   *Royal GS, High Wycombe*
C Gottlieb   *Manchester GS*
J Goulding   *King Edward's S, Birmingham*
S J Greenwood   *King Edward's Camp Hill Boys S*
I A Greig   *Dulwich C*
S Handyside   *Newstead Wood S*
Z Harris   *McCauley S*
M Hayward   *St Gregory's S*
K P Heath   *St George's C*
P Heslop   *Repton S*
R Hiadky   *Chesterton Community C*
K Hill   *Rathmore GS*
N Hills   *Marlwood S*

M Holt *Chesterton Community C*
N Homer *Minster S*
P Hoodless *Central Newcastle HS*
S Howard *Haberdashers Askes Girls S*
C Howe *Repton S*
C Hu *Cheltenham Ladies C*
J Hynes *Downside S*
L Islam *Haberdashers Askes Girls S*
O James *Millfield S*
S James *Conyers S*
C Jennings *Merchant Taylors S*
C John *St Paul's Girls S*
A Johnson *St Paul's Girls S*
C Jones *Aylesbury HS*
C Jones *Holmes Chapel CS*
K Kanji *Dulwich C*
C Kelly *St Ivo S*
S Kingston *George Abbot S*
P Kissacu *Queen Elizabeth II HS*
S Klemba *Nottingham HS*
M J Knight *Uppingham S*
T Knowles *St John's S*
A Laher *St Paul's S*
M J Lang *Dulwich C*
N Laud *Northgate HS*
M Lewis *King Edward's S, Birmingham*
T Litt *Dr Challoners GS*
S Mahmood *St Paul's S*
C Mallock *Oakham S*
A Mankikar *St Christopher's S*
S Marcer *Wirral GS*
C Marples *Bishop Rawstorne S*
S Mathieson *Glyn S*
P McCarthy *Dame Alice Owens S*
R McCawley *Bolton S Girls Division*
D McLean *Grosvenor HS*
T Miers *St Paul's Girls S*
S Mohan *Dulwich C*
Moorthy *Dulwich C*
D Morgan *Merchant Taylors S*
G Morgan *King Edward's Camp Hill Boys S*
S J Morgan *Queen Elizabeth's Hospital*
G W F Morris *Royal GS, Worcester*
M Naylor *Holmes Chapel CS*
A Neubert *Monks Park S*
D Nicholls *Merchiston Castle S*
M Nightingale *King Edward's S, Birmingham*
G Oates *Grange S*
R C Patel *Hurstpeirpoint C*
J Patterson *Haydon Bridge HS*
A Peck *Winchester C*
D Penny *Droitwich HS*
A Phillips *Rawlett S*

P Phillips *Madras C*
S Pollard *Cheltenham Ladies C*
L Porter *Bath HS*
I Potter *Conyers S*
J Price *Dr Challoners GS*
K Probst *City of London Girls S*
W Ramsay *Trinity S*
E Reid *Charterhouse*
S Richardson *Golborne Girls S*
F Robertson *King Edward's S, Handsworth*
A Romanelli *Royal Latin S*
C Routh *Skipton Girls HS*
C Rozzeck *Herts & Essex HS*
A Sarangi *Repton Prep S*
A Sarkar *Winchester C*
J Scholey *Monmouth S*
C Scott *St Paul's Girls S*
J Scurlock *Minster S*
C Seanor *Hull Girls HS*
K Shelley *Ardingly College JS*
F Shelton *Bishopshalt S*
C Sherratt *Dr Challoners GS*
F Shilling *Walthamstow Hall*
P Shippey *Whitburn CS*
J Skeet *Royal GS, Worcester*
R A Skevington *Royal GS, Worcester*
H Sleeth *Wirral GS*
D Spiby *King Edward's Camp Hill Boys S*
R Springle *St Bedes S*
A Stamp *Ipswich S*
J Swindells *Aylesbury HS*
S Tang *Bishopshalt S*
R J A Taylor *Lord Wandsworth C*
H Thomas *Broxbourne S*
N Tuckey *Bedford S*
R Turner *Wellington S*
C Uffindel *Berkhamsted Girls S*
B Utenthal *Abingdon S*
R Vincent *Newstead Wood S*
J Walton *City of London S*
R Walton *Dr Challoners GS*
S Waters *Bedford S*
C Waterson *St Louis GS*
D Ainsley Watson *Winchester C*
A Weaver *Dr Challoners GS*
S Wells *King Edward's S, Stratford*
N Westerdale *Dr Challoners GS*
B Weston *King Alfred S*
S Woolston *Trinity S*
M Worthington *Stubbington House S*
G J Wright *Shrewsbury S*
J Young *King Edward's S, Birmingham*

UK JMO awards: 1989

The 1989 paper was experimental, and was deliberately too demanding. There were nevertheless some excellent scripts, even though candidates certainly found the questions challenging! Three candidates, who produced seven or eight good solutions, were essentially *Gold medallists*; nine, who produced five or six good solutions, were *Silver medallists*; and 40 students, who managed three or four good solutions, were *Bronze medallists*.

Gold medallists

Angela Barnes   *King Edward's HS, Birmingham*
Henry Braun   *Dulwich C*
David Winter   *St Paul's S*

Silver medallists

S Ball   *City of London S*
S D Boyd   *King Edward's S, Birmingham*
T Budds   *City of London S*
T J Gershon   *Dr Challoners GS*
S Kumaran   *St Paul's S*
J Longley   *St Lawrence C*
D M Pooley   *Impington Village C*
D A Smith   *Arnold S*
T Yasoki   *Sherborne S*

Bronze medallists

R Beaty   *St Clement's HS*
J C N Beck   *Whitgift S*
S Binnie   *Royal Latin S*
R J H Birtwhistle   *Winchester C*
P M Carpenter   *Queen Elizabeth's Hospital*
R Chaudhary   *Bishops Stortford C*
E Ciampa   *City of London S*
T E Dent   *King Edward's S, Birmingham*
M Dove   *Alleynes HS*
J A Dummett   *Winchester C*
G A Duncan   *Royal GS, Newcastle*
M Farrow   *Dulwich C*

M R Fernandes   *Clifton C*
T Finnis   *Bedford S*
A J Forster   *Queen Elizabeth's Hospital*
S Glover   *Oakham S*
C Gutteridge   *Ventnor Middle S*
E R Haines   *Winchester C*
A Hickman   *Royal GS, High Wycombe*
S M Lee   *King Edward's Camp Hill Boys S*
P D Martin   *Hampton S*
G F H Massiah   *Loughborough GS*
A Mehendale   *Whitgift S*
M Mitchell   *St Peter's RC S*
K O'Connor   *Hitchin Boys S*
G O'Shaughnessy   *Heathfield HS*
L J Odell   *Perse S for Girls*
M L Peat   *Park View CS*
M Perrie   *King Edward's Camp Hill Boys S*
D P I Pierce Price   *City of London S*
L L A Price   *Bury GS*
P Scott   *Millfield S*
R M Taylor   *Hampton S*
M Thomas   *Millthorpe S*
A P Turnbull   *Winchester C*
D N Wake   *King Edward's S, Birmingham*
A Wayman   *Ampleforth C*
B J Wilson   *Winchester C*
T Woodhouse   *Holgate S*